TECHNOLOGY ASSESSMENT AND QUALITY OF LIFE

TECHNOLOGY ASSESSMENT

AND

QUALITY OF LIFE

PROCEEDINGS OF THE 4th GENERAL CONFERENCE OF

SAINT

(Salzburg Assembly: Impact of the New Technology)

HELD AT SCHLOSS LEOPOLDSKRON, SALZBURG, AUSTRIA
SEPTEMBER 24–28, 1972

Edited by

GERHARD J. STÖBER and DIETER SCHUMACHER

Elsevier Scientific Publishing Company

Amsterdam · London · New York 1973

ELSEVIER SCIENTIFIC PUBLISHING COMPANY
335 Jan van Galenstraat
P.O. Box 1270, Amsterdam, The Netherlands

AMERICAN ELSEVIER PUBLISHING COMPANY, INC.
52 Vanderbilt Avenue
New York, New York 10017

The Editors:

GERHARD J. STÖBER

President of SAINT and Director, SYSTEMPLAN eV.
Institut für Umweltforschung und Entwicklungsplanung
Tiergartenstrasse 15, Heidelberg, Federal Republic of Germany

DIETER SCHUMACHER

Chairman of the SAINT Conference on Technology Assessment
and Quality of Life and Director, SYSTEMPLAN e.V.
Institut für Umweltforschung und Entwicklungsplanung
Tiergartenstrasse 15, Heidelberg, Federal Republic of Germany

Library of Congress Card Number: 73-77071

ISBN 0-444-41137-2

With 26 illustrations and 17 tables.

Printed in The Netherlands

PREFACE

It was in the beginning of October 1971 in Heidelberg, when the General Assembly of SAINT (Salzburg Assembly: Impact of the New Technology) at its annual meeting decided to hold the next General SAINT Conference on the Theme „Technology Assessment and Quality of Life". In choosing this subject, SAINT wanted to make a contribution to define the interrelationships between two new key terms brought up in the political and scientific arena, and to identify the social role and the genuine political function of technology assessment.

The Conference was held on September 24 – 28, 1972 at Schloss Leopoldskron, Salzburg, Austria, with about 60 participants from ten European countries and the United States, bringing together technologists as well as social scientists, researchers and planners, model builders and pragmatists, and other experienced people from different disciplines and societal institutions.

Parallel to this Conference, but with some connection and mutual participation, a NATO Summer Institute on Technology Assessment, based on collaboration with the International Institute for the Management of Technology in Milan and the National Science Foundation, took place at Gargnano, Italy. Earlier in 1972, OECD had invited a number of experts from member countries to discuss methodologies and opportunities of technology assessment implementation. Also, the International Society for Technology Assessment was founded in that period, 'a world membership organization serving as both a bridge and a forum for a broad spectrum of disciplines, organizations and constituencies which can contribute to the structuring, study, control and resolution of the world's technological challenges, dilemmas and opportunities'.

All these efforts have prepared the scene for a wider discussion on how the concept and instruments of technology assessment can be introduced into public policy making for an effective control of technical change and the benefit of a well-balanced, quality-oriented social development. Better knowledge on this field of concern is of vital importance for all those countries which try to operationalize and institutionalize technology assessment within governmental and private sectors.

This book is intended to present to a wider audience the Papers given at the Salzburg Conference, including a short introduction to the Conference Theme and two critical reviews on the discussions prepared by participants. Unfortunately, J. Mak's excellent contribution on „The Quality of Life and Organizational Strategies of the Industrial Enterprise" could not be included in this volume because of the serious illness of the author which made it impossible for him to prepare his paper in time.

The Executive Committee of SAINT and the Editors have made efforts for a rapid publication. They, therefore, have to apologize for any remaining shortcomings in the editing. Nevertheless, they hope that this series of papers will stimulate further discussions on the use of technology assessment for improving quality of life both in the scientific community and in the practical field of governmental and industrial bodies.

We would like to express our gratitude to our colleagues, the authors, who helped us a lot and who keep responsibility for the views expressed in their individual contributions. We also wish to thank Elsevier Publishing Company, Amsterdam, and Gebr. Angerer GmbH, Weinheim, Germany, for the pleasant and fruitful cooperation during the production period. Last but not least, acknowledgements are due to Ingrid Casaretto and Christa Wetzel from the SYSTEMPLAN Institute in Heidelberg for their invaluable technical assistance.

Heidelberg and Salford, Lancashire, February 1973

| Gerhard J. Stöber | Louis Turner | Dieter Schumacher |
| President of SAINT | Secretary of SAINT | Conference Chairman |

TECHNOLOGY ASSESSMENT AND QUALITY OF LIFE

CONTENTS

8

9

Introduction

INTRODUCTION TO THE CONFERENCE THEME

AND

OVERVIEW OF THE PROCEEDINGS

Gerhard J. Stöber and Dieter Schumacher
SYSTEMPLAN e.V.
Institut für Umweltforschung und Entwicklungsplanung
Heidelberg, Federal Republic of Germany

A wide public disenchantment with new technologies (accused of causing our principal environmental disasters) and the permanent dissatisfaction of individuals, groups and mankind as to their standards and circumstances of living (vaguely and comprehensively described by the new catchword 'quality of life') are the main roots of the topic for this Conference.

It is now almost a commonplace that technologies *have* caused major damages and disequilibria in our various environments and social systems. It seems, on the other hand, that there is no effective alternative to the continued use of technologies (new and old ones) in the future, except that a wiser concept for their development and application is highly desirable and essential for securing the further viability of human societies.

Technology assessment, i.e. putting values to technologies, is feasible only if there is a source of values, a 'reference board', in the light of which the impact of technologies may be monitored and controlled, in order to transform technology development into a *dependent* variable of social choices and change. If we had a unanimous notion of what quality of life should be like, technology assessment would be relatively easy to perform. However, there are different, more or less promising ways of describing, measuring and experiencing quality of life, and there are also numerous alternative solutions to cure quality deficiencies: Technologies are only one type of means, one resource out of many to be activated for problem solving.

Thus, the bridge between technology assessment and quality of life is twofold:

— Quality of life criteria and standards help to identify deficiency areas (problems) of our environmental and social systems, i.e. areas that need (political) action for improvement, which in turn implies a screening of the main causes (technological or other ones) of these deficiencies.

— Quality of life objectives and requirements set the scene for designing alternative solutions and development strategies for the future, including and activating, hopefully in an optimum mix, combinations of technological as well as other resources.

Certainly, the term 'quality of life' needs clarification. So far, it is nothing but a 'theme', a catchword which has entered the political scene. We have to avoid the impression that it could eventually stand for a 'recipe' of how to achieve a certain standard of living.

Is quality of life just a new term for satisfying living conditions (for which mankind has strived for centuries) or is it something which can be delivered to human settlements by a definable set of facilities? Is it something that could eventually be designed beforehand (anticipating a beneficial impact) or is it something which develops (or not) in human settlements as time passes? Is it a phenomenon with a static, inchangeable hard core, or a highly dynamic category, changing its content in short, medium, and long range time intervals? Is it measurable or does any quantitative description harm the true issue in so far as the phenomena to be described become highly distorted? These are some of the essentials to be looked at during this Conference, but certainly too complex to be answered within a few days.

In several introductory papers, the two dimensions of the theme, namely technology assessment *(Dieter Schumacher)* and quality of life *(Gerhard J. Stöber)*, are being somewhat prestructured to gain better access to the complex of open questions and to assess our present state of the art and the knowledge available. *Clark C. Abt* and *Francois Hetman* then are looking at the interrelationships and linkages between social and technical systems and how to achieve a new attitude of social committment in technology development. It was argued that the unit-oriented way of thinking, concentrating too early on subsystems (which people like!) and our limited capability in understanding more complex systems are the predominant pitfalls. The key questions raised here read as follows:

- How do technical systems become more sensible to human and social needs?

- How to design systems that really change qualities in wishful directions?

Contributions of *John Hall* and of *Gert v. Kortzfleisch* (not published in this volume) went into some detail as to how quality-of-life-categories can be operationalized analytically and empirically. This delicate issue is probably the main 'problem area' of technology assessment itself: On the one hand there is the need for quantitative or at least clearly described qualitative indicators which can stand for particular qualities. On the other hand, we have not yet learned how to aggregate relevant data, as collected on the individual's, group or community level, without violating the nature of this information. Clearly, neither existing statistical data *alone* nor primary empirical investigations *alone* will provide us with quality of life-performance and expectation standards representative for the society or parts of it. We need ways and means to synthesize quality of life 'descriptions' from complementary data coming from different sources *including* statistical services, opinion polls, group discussions, intensive interviews, observations, etc.

In looking more systematically at the various phases of technology development and here again at the roles and social impacts of technologies, the following sub-themes were approached:

1) The Development and Dissemination of New Technologies — Their Positive and Negative Aspects Regarding Quality of Life.

    Besides the basic papers of *Clark C. Abt* and *Francois Hetman,* this theme was taken up by *Nadezda Grubor* looking at the international dissemination and transfer aspects, and by *Peter Milling* who bridged the gap towards the Club of Rome results relevant to technology development. *Clark C. Abt's* game (not published in this volume) on how to improve the quality of life in countries of different stages of development broadened the view of the participants and the discussion to a worldwide dimension.

2) The Process of Industrial and Agricultural Production and its Impact on Quality on Life.

Here, the problems associated with the process of production of goods, based on the use of new technology, were covered. In the first part of this section, several speakers reviewed the structural changes of work and the quality of work conditions, *James S. Wilson* reporting on a local case study of the British shipyard industry, *Rudolph A. C. Bruyns* looking at the impact of work and environment on work motivation, *John Leslie-Miller* analyzing relevant processes in multinational companies, and *Johannes Mak* (not published in this volume) drawing up relationships between the quality of (working) life and organizational strategies for industrial enterprises.

The second part focussed on external effects of production and their impact on environment, with contributions by *Manfred Fischer* related to industrial pollution and by *Jürgen Reichling* dealing with the prospects of food production and quality of food.

3) Assessing the Distribution, Application and Consumption of New Technologies.

Apart from the pre-production-phase where technologies originally are developed and disseminated, and from the process of industrial production, technology affects quality of life a third time when new products being distributed and used within society finally come to markets or quasi-markets. *Robert Rea* and *Paul Drewe* gave examples, based on technology assessment case studies and social cost-benefit-approaches, on how quality of life and technology aspects may be incorporated into urban and regional planning and development, with special regard to spatial infrastructure as a major recepient and multiplier of technology application and consumption. The latter context was also illustrated in a paper given by *Horst D. Supe* (not published in this volume).

In turning to more practical and operational aspects, transportation problems were taken as a field for testing the concept of social committment, in organizing the match between new technological opportunities and unmet social needs and desirabilities. *Anders G. Ejerhed* gave a report on the transportation planning for the Stockholm metropolitan area, *Dieter Haseke* presented a new generation of transportation systems for the future, and *Robin Roy* introduced simulation techniques as a tool to penetrate this complex part of the public service system.

A final, very essential aspect of the Conference theme, namely the effective organization for social problem-oriented technology assessment, paved the way for drawing conclusions. There are, of course, numerous ways and degrees of assuming a partial or full responsibility for social committment in government, science and industry. However, no general set of recommendations as to how effective institutionalization could be performed exists so far *Dieter Altenpohl* on the one side and *Horst Geschka* and *Götz R. Schaude* on the other, adopted quite different views on how industry should and could become prepared for assessment tasks. *Dieter Schumacher* demonstrated that also governments and public administrations resemble quite specific organizational environments, requiring individual design for each particular scene.

While it is admittedly hard to come to 'conclusions' at a Conference, particularly in such a vast area of knowledge and concern, the Conference programme was structured in a way which 'automatically' touched upon all aspects vital to the main theme during the course of the meeting. Thus, although opinions and reactions were quite heterogeneous, the participants were united in following jointly the thread through the subject, giving rise to a high degree of argumentation and interaction. *Brian Wynne* and *Louis Turner* assumed the task of reviewing independently from each other the discourse as they saw it at the closure of the Conference. Their reports and syntheses reflect in an excellent manner the stimulating spirit of the Conference, the wide range of thoughts and engagement present, and the critical views dominating the deliberations.

The Display of the Problem Landscape

QUALITY OF LIFE – ITS SCOPE AND ELEMENTS

Gerhard J. Stöber
SYSTEMPLAN e. V.
Institut für Umweltforschung und Entwicklungsplanung
Heidelberg, Federal Republic of Germany

1. Quality of Life: Fashionable Slogan or More?

Since about two, three years we are living with a new term. A strong and peculiar fascination seems to proceed from it. This new magic word is called 'Quality of Life'. Both the scientific community and the political arena have taken possession of it, it has become the subject of many discussions and programmatic speeches, but up to now relatively little solid work has been invested in getting under the surface of the concept and to cheer up and to structure its content systematically.

In spring of this year the Industriegewerkschaft Metall, i.e. the German Metal Workers Union, held a big international congress on 'Quality of Life: Challenge of the Future'. On this occasion the German Federal Minister for Economic Cooperation, Erhard Eppler, expressed his opinion, namely that the term Quality of Life would mark a break-through on the way from economic to ecological thinking, to new measures of political actioning, and would create its own dynamics. Hitherto, there is some evidence that he was right. However, it will depend decisively on our efforts to operationalize the fascinating slogan for the purpose of practical policy-making, whether it will prove sound enough to introduce a reorientation of our systems of values, objectives and actions, or whether it will initiate at best a series of academic papers and essays which rarely can move something concrete in the political and social reality.

As we know from experience, quite frequently meaningful concepts which in the beginning are euphorically accepted, meet very soon again with indifference, pragmatically veiled disregard, or even strong aversions, even before they can really stand the test. More or less the same happened, for example, with terms like systems analysis, policy planning, innovation, participation, democratization, futurology, ecology, environment, or the word 'Urbanität' which was newly brought up in Germany about 12 years ago.

The emergence of the debate on Quality of Life is without doubt signaling the opening of a new dimension in the attitudes of society and in our reflections on the conditions of human existence and development. It indicates the transition to a more differentiated and more subtile assessment of the living circumstances we have produced. It offers the chance for a more enlightened policy of societal change, a policy which is oriented more closely towards the needs and expectations of man both as an individual human being and as part of the society surrounded by limited natural resources. It is based on the growing understanding that some of the goals and measures towards which, up to now, we have primarily adjusted our doings, are today becoming obsolete or at least insufficient if we want to secure the overcoming, the preservation of the status quo, or even the social progress of society at all levels.

2. Why Talking about Quality of Life?

The public awareness of existing and potential problems has initiated the discussion on Quality of Life-topics. We talk about Quality of Life because our optimistic belief in progress is beginning to stagger, because we have developed some serious doubts that increasing quantity, measured in terms of more people, more material goods and installations, higher gross national product, more and also more efficient technologies are still positively correlated to quality in the sense of the degree of satisfaction of individual needs and of social welfare requirements. We talk about Quality of Life because we are perceiving the loss of quality which — with regard to the exploitation of nature and man by more and more men — has occured, or the appearence of which must be feared. People begin to understand that the world — in any case still for a fairly long period of time — is finite and its resources are limited. They are becoming sensitive to the fact that the creation and production of new goods as well as the consequent application of new technical means in the societal process of their economic utilization has indeed solved certain problems, but has also necessarily created or will create in the future other and often bigger problems elsewhere.

The catchword Quality of Life did not enter public discussion because of the setting up of new, positive goals for society, but mainly because of the perceptible existence of negative qualities, namely those problems and deficiencies which have accumulated as consequences of earlier man-made decisions and activities.

Looking back one can say that the question of quality was at first brought up by the so-called ecological crisis, i.e. the threat, damage, and destruction of components of our natural environment in the 'vicious circle of demography, economy and technology'. The discussion on the quality of the natural environment, however, emanating from the problems of the physical pollution of water, air, and soil, was quickly broadened when one began to question whether the artificially made environment, e.g. our cities and infrastructure installations, could be left out, if the discourse is dealing with men's environment. There was the indisputable argument that the urban environment built by men and for which year by year — with dubious results — tremendous sums of money are invested, has principally the same importance for the personal development of a human being as a part of original nature.

On this basis, only a small third step, which in fact occurred nearly simultaneously, was consequently necessary to widen once again the prevalent scope of quality. From now on the very comprehensive question, simply referring to the quality of life came into the focus of discussion. The question implies that, fundamentally speaking, no aspect or element which might be relevant for the satisfaction of material, physical, psychical, and intellectual needs and requirements, can be disregarded, neither the social environment within the family, at the place of work, at school, and in the public, nor questions regarding the procurement of employment, income distribution, old-age pension systems, access to information or participation in decision-making and so forth.

We find ourselves in quite a difficult position. On the one hand, we are confronted with a huge complex of expectations and public tasks aiming at improving quality of life, on the other hand we do not know precisely which substantial qualities really constitute 'the' quality of life (and for whom), and how it can be measured.

3. On the Necessity to Improve the Knowledge on Quality of Life

In the present situation it seems to me a question of absolutely no importance whether quality of life could or should be measured *as a whole*. This would raise very difficult problems of aggregating partial qualities at first, and before we do not sufficiently know how to express and to measure these, the fiction of a total quality of life-index is a real second order affair.

Although one should not loose time in seeking *the* general indicator which might allow an adequate measurement of quality of life-degrees, it should be emphasized again that quality of life *has* to be seen as an entity, composed of many and very different realities which contribute — directly or indirectly, more or less, positively or negatively, in a complementary or substitutive relationship — to the overall quality of life conditions of an individual, a group or a society as a whole. The quality of life of a particular urban environment from the individual point of view e.g. does of course not only depend on the possession of a roomy dwelling, the accessibility of public and private services, and the availabity of fresh air and clean water. Let us consider a human being whose needs are completely satisfied with the exception of, let us say, the need for social contacts. We can assume that his total quality of life is not simply reduced by the factor loneliness, but presumably has to be classified lower, because of the effect, that the absence of a vital component will also impair other existing qualities. Health e.g. as one very important part of quality of life is not only determined by hygienically sufficient housing conditions but also depends on the quality of food, the social relations within the family, the stresses and risks at the place of work, etc.

Another most relevant question is how to structure the total spectrum of quality of life-components adequately: It seems a bit too simple and even somewhat trivial to split up the total scope of quality of life rashly and thoughtlessly into quality-fields or -areas respectively, such as housing, clothing, nutrition, urban transport, water supply and so forth, without making thorough considerations and conducting systematic studies on a satisfying definition, delimitation and structuring of possible fields of quality. Several attempts have been undertaken by different authors, however, most of the approaches available so far are looking fairly poor. They may perhaps be suitable to stimulate discussion, but not to establish a stringent and coherent framework for a careful, subtle description of quality of life.

Let us suppose that we have defined a well-structured system of psychologically-based, need-oriented quality fields covering the spheres of production, consumption, ecological and social organization in their broader meaning. The following question must then be, in which conceivable realities the qualities of life manifest themselves. In other words: What are the concrete situations and conditions which may express the quality of life under consideration? This principal question has, of course, to be seen separated from the fact that the same components are not relevant to everybody, and that, again, the relevant components are normally evaluated differently by different people.

The systematic search for quality components (e. g. access to open space for the inhabitant of a particular urban settlement) has to be distinguished from the identification of those concrete conditions from which a specific quality is derived, and from the further question, which measurable variables — and now I have in mind the so-called indicators — are available or could be defined in order to make these conditions describable ore even calculable. This would mean, if we take the example mentioned above, that one has to ask what in fact accessibility denotes. Again another question is, which factors, forces, tools, etc. produce, influence or determine a particular, well-described quality. For practical purposes we should distinguish at least between quality-components, quality-indicators, and quality-determinants.

Quality of life is certainly not what scientists imagine it could or should be. What higher quality of life is cannot be decreed by small groups of knowledgable and better informed experts. Quality of life is what people regard as quality of life. The quality of life-potential and -profile of a city e.g. cannot simply be expressed by a set of infrastructure equipment-characteristics or other types of indicators, but depends on what people perceive and evaluate as their quality of life. For that reason we have to distrust all attempts to elaborate quality of life-schemes and to classify quality of life components without taking notice of empirical data on the structure of needs and expectations of people, divided into relevant social groups.

We could ask each participant of this conference to present, from his personal point of view, a list of the 10 to 20 most important components in the range of their quality of life-expectations, and perhaps also a list containing the main problems society would have to cope with in order to fulfil these expectations. Quite probably the outcome of such a test would be a most heterogeneous pattern of categories, located at quite different levels of aggregation, involving a lot of unidentified conflicts, let alone a different weighting of the possible quality criteria as well as of the different evaluation − according to these criteria − of the real world situation.

Things do not become easier if we consider that quality of life cannot be seen only in an individual or in a group perspective, but must be approached as well from the society's (or better: political) as from the planner's point of view. The necessity of the society's point of view is evident because of the immanent incompatibilities existing between partial qualities and between the qualities of life for the different social groups. This leads to the problem of decision-making and the setting of priorities, in other words, of evaluation and selection of alternative choices. The policy planner's point of view is of importance because of the fact, that higher quality of life is normally not the direct consequence of one political decision and a corresponding number of actions, but can only be realized by a long series of interwoven and complementary initiatives, programmes and projects, the elaboration and implementation of which needs efficient organization and complex mechanisms. Many of them merely have a very mediate connection to the concrete range of experience of an individual human being.

4. General Requirements for Improving Quality of Life

This statement is a part of the introduction to the conference theme. Its function is mainly to raise some principal questions and to restrict them to a few comments which could help to provide a certain frame for the orientation of the following papers and discussions. Before we turn to the role of technology for quality of life and, more specifically, to concentrate on the function of technology assessment in this context, I should like to draw the attention very briefly to the general prerequisites for any improvement of the quality of life. They could be ascribed to three headings: Information, resources and organization. In each of these big pertinant areas serious deficiencies and bottle-necks must be seen.

The information problem, which is perhaps the cardinal one, includes three topics: Without operational knowledge on 1. possible scopes and elements, and existing potentials and profiles of quality of life, 2. positive and negative impacts on quality of life and their direct and indirect dependences, and, 3. potential quality of life-objectives and -standards, the formulation of suitable policies can hardly be expected.

Without the availability of adequate resources, and here we have to think not only in terms of financial means but also of personnel, of industrial and infrastructure capacities, of land, and — not as least — technology, no significant improvement of our living conditions will be attainable.

Finally it has to be emphasized that nothing really will move towards better quality of life for people if there is no sufficient organization for inter- and intra-sectorial planning, decision-making and implementation of policy actions within government and public administration at all levels.

We need both, a problem- and action-oriented view on quality of life, and for the benefit of this none of the three requirements can be ignored.

5. How to Get Operational Knowledge on Quality of Life?

In order to lay the groundwork for better policy-planning one has to go down from the sky of general philosophical concepts on quality of life to the bottom of practically applicable knowledge. It has become more and more a common opinion that the key to a better understanding and management of the whole quality of life-issue is the development of social indicators. Social indicators are tools which can help us to describe, measure and assess performance in many social areas. Properly and meaningfully designed, they allow to operationalize complex quality of life-phenomena, -problems and -goals, to define the primary and secondary impact of certain actions and developments on well-described qualities, and to identify their costs and benefits. All these elements should, by using social indicators, be prepared for deliberate rating.

In practice, this is at least the best idea, however, the setting up of useful social indicators proved to be extremely difficult, and it seems that our efforts are still at the very beginning.

One should also mention here that it is not satisfying to collect more or less extended catalogues of social indicators, many of them perhaps just taken by chance. The problem is rather to develop coherent systems of indicators which are linked together in such a way that the reality of quality of life with its manifold implications and the mechanisms of change become transparent and can be adequately structured.

The present state of the art in quality of life-research is, as far as I can see, nothing to write home about. It is characterized on the one hand by a few experimental studies which in principal try to cope with the whole spectrum of quality of life-domaines in a quite pragmatical manner and on a relatively high level of aggregation. On the other hand there is the immense number of those studies and surveys which are often performed totally isolated from each other, concentrating on sectorally and/or regionally limited aspects of quality of life. The low instrumental quality of the knowledge produced so far is mainly due to the bad organization and coordination of these many research efforts, to their methodological deficiencies and to the fact that scientists still have too slight insights into the practical information needs at the front of political decision making and public administration.

6. The Two Faces of Technology Regarding Quality of Life

Since Clark Abt in the following contribution will deal more deeply with the social role of technology, I can restrict myself again to a few introductory sentences just to get the connexion to the second dimension of our general subject. It is a commonplace that technology has many close relations with quality of life. It was already mentioned that the whole question of quality of life actually came up as a consequence of technology, i.e. its application in society. For a couple of years the discussion tended to polarize again and again into two contradictory ideological directions.

The optimistic faith in the usefulness and absolute necessity of new technology as such for enabling societal change and social progress was defined as the typical attitude of people of the first position. Growing resistance against technological innovation because of the negative impacts of new technologies on man, society and the environment, in other words on quality of life, is the characteristic of the second position.

Both positions are too coarse-grained to be right or useful. None of them can help us to solve the problems of today's and tomorrow's society. Of course many of the problems of deterioration of quality of life are caused by the use and misuse of technology. However, there are also other origins for quality of life-problems. What we regard as problems, depends on our values and value systems, and only a part of this is reflecting basic individual and social needs. The changing of values could also change or even eliminate problems. Nevertheless it seems evident that most of the problems of decreasing quality of life will not disappear with changing our value systems. The existing as well as the potential problems we are confronted with require solutions, to speak more precisely, packages of institutional, organizational, financial, and also technical measures etc. Meanwhile our problems are of a nature, particularly in terms of size and complexity that one can no longer dispense with the contribution of technology in order to solve technology-induced problems. Thus technology must be seen from both sides of the coin, the bad side showing technology as a quality-decreasing problem generator, the good side giving us hope that the capacity of technology could be used as an instrument for the improvement of quality of life, provided that this use is guided and controlled wiser than in the past.

The concept of technology assessment claims to appease the controverse attitudes against technology mentioned above. It is expected to take the due step towards a humanization of science and technology. Technology assessment essentially is tantamount to the evaluation and selection of alternative technologies with regard to a clear-defined set of objectives and potential applications. It is designed to take deliberately into account the short-, middle-, and long-range effects of technological application including its physical, psychological, economic, social and political side-effects which very often are connected only indirectly with the actual use of technology.

But again, technology assessment must not be misunderstood as a refusal of advanced technologies and their application. It has not merely to do with saying 'No' to socially undesirable technological applications but just as well with saying 'Yes' to those technologies the supply and setting-free of which could bring us nearer to a better quality of life.

THE SOCIAL ROLE OF TECHNOLOGY

Clark C. Abt
Abt Associates Inc.
Cambridge, Massachusetts, U.S.A.

There is today a deepening pessimism concerning the social role of technology. The number of students seeking engineering degrees has dropped. Reform politicians accuse governments of neglect of the poor while spending heavily on technology. Weapons of war and the defenses against them — always heavily technological — taint technology itself as murderous. Not only does technology have a destructive image now, it even has a faintly squalid one: In the U. S. today, of thousands of unemployed aerospace engineers, many are being retrained for careers in public service, dentistry, and commerce.

Transportation, power, extraction, and production technologies are viewed by the public as principal polluters. Computers are seen as dehumanizing. Mass media are feared as purveyors of cheap commercialism, incentives to violence, and subliminal political propagandizers. Drugs legal and illegal ruin the lives of housewives and alienated youth.

Are these concerns justified by the facts? At least in part, they seem to be. As Table A summarizes, *technology is still too unit — rather than systems-oriented,* despite ironically the technologists being our most competent systems analysts and designers. But, partly out of historical momentum, partly from economic and political pressures, *technological advances are often advances in the unit at the expense of the system —* and I mean that in the sense of not only the technical problem but also for the political economy. The negative side effects rarely overwhelm the positive achievements: most people would still prefer to drive cars and have air pollution and traffic jams and accidents.

Nevertheless, the negative side effects are growing faster, and more mutually supportively, than the positive results of technology, and that is widely sensed and feared.

Table A: Technology is still too unit — rather than systems-oriented

Sector	Major Technological Change	Unit Payoff	Unanticipated System Cost	Impact on Qualities of Life
Health	Antibiotics	greater survial of infections	increasing development of resistant strains	+ reduced disease mortality − risk of suddenly increased mortality
Education	Cheap textbooks Programmed instruction	wider access to printed litera-ture. Self-teaching economics	fragmentation of cul-ture decline in quality of teachers	+ diversity of choices, self-development − entertainment and self-deve-lopment from great teachers
Entertainment: Films Books TV Music/Records	Cheap home audio-visual entertainment	widened access to A-V material	superficial entertain-ment crowds out high quality	+ democratization of culture-wider access + home education opportuni-ties − violence and trivia on TV may reduce public mental health − vulnerability to propaganda & loss of freedom
Housing	Cheap high rise building construction	lower unit physi-cal production cost	'vertical slums' crowding, social patho-logy	+ higher purely physical quali-ty − lower social quality − privacy, quiet
Transport	Trailer Cheap cars	low cost family enjoyment of na-ture individual mobi-lity	ugly trailer parks traffic jams, air pollu-tion, land use waste	+ cheap enjoyment of nature for a few − quantitative pollution of trailer parks + mobility, freedom − quiet, clean air, safety
Agriculture	Cheap chemical ferti-lizers	higher yield per acre, better crops	pollution of ground water	*short-run* + reduced cost of food − pollution of bays and rivers − tax costs of clean-ups and substitute methods
Manufacturing	Automated production line	higher unit pro-ductivity and worker income	boring jobs, exclusive 'worker elite' protective against redistribution	+ decreased working hours − job dissatisfaction

In the last 25 years the United States alone has spent over $200 billion on R & D, with over 80% of this devoted to military, atomic energy, and space efforts not directly responsive to major social needs. This is probably history's greatest socially irresponsible investment in technology since the pyramids. If most of that $160 billion had been spent on medical research, education, housing, transportation, environment, etc., I wonder if the United States would not be a much better country today, and even more secure though less well armed.

In this gathering *crisis of the perceived social role of technology,* there are three major alternatives in the immediate future:

A. *Continued and increasing public disenchantment* with technology, followed by reduced public support and self-fulfilling prophecies of technological inefficiency;

B. *Polarization* of opinion into technocratic and antitechnocratic factions with great loss of potential useful applications;

C. *Redirection* of technology from military and nonmilitary nationalistic glorification to urgent social roles in health, nutrition, housing, environment, education, law enforcement, etc.

I believe we are observing a race between the trend toward the successful social application of technology and the trends of public alienation with technology. I fear that if there is a widespread disillusion with the hopes for technology, scientific thought itself will not long be free and supported, and some dark ages may be upon us.

What does this threat mean to scientists, technologists, and technology planners and managers? First, *technologists need to develop rapport with and learn from social scientists what the major felt social needs are,* and perhaps to become at least amateur social scientists themselves. Second, *technologists must not give up being technologists,* because technology cannot be applied to social problems if there is no technology continually being developed. Third, *technologists need to become sensitive to quality of life impacts,* unintended or not, of major technological changes, and to determine if such impacts are consistent with a publicly acceptable social role for technology.

To learn what the major perceived social needs are, one needs only to examine the copious literature of contemporary social research. In the United States today, the Federal government spends over $200 million per year, regardless of politics, on such research. The Federal Departments of Health, Education, and Welfare, Housing and Urban Development, Labour, Transportation, Office of Economic Opportunity, and most of the corresponding departments in the 50 states continually research social and economic needs of the population, develop and plan alternative action programs, and evaluate program processes, outputs, and impacts. Most of the problem-solving technologies developed in the course of hardware technology R & D are applied. Some of these are systems analysis and design, econometrics, decision modeling, sampling and statistics, industrial psychology, and organizational development. (See Table B)

But the interest must be there for the technologist to assume an active and benign social role. Technology today is too interdependent with politics, economics, and social change for the technologist to assume that all will continue as before if he simply does his assigned job. If he is socially responsible, he must take some responsibility for the social applications and quality of life impacts of his technology. He cannot take the attitude of the scientific attache of a major European nation who said to me, „In my country, there *are* no social problems!"

Yet the technologist must retain his expertise. If it is true, as many scientific and engineering educators, managers, and planners claim, that only with technology can we solve our social and economic problems, then it is essential to retain technologists as such. Even if it is *not* true, or only partly true, then we must still have technological expertise simply to control and minimize the negative impacts of the technology we already have and cannot help continuing to produce because it is an intrinsic and inseparable part of modern economic civilization.

If the socially productive technologist of the future is to remain an expert technologist while he also must become at least an amateur social scientist, how can he find the time to do both? I believe the time is both available and needs to be used thus. The individual life time is available as medical technology makes up to 50% increases in working

Table B: Some Problem-Solving Technologies

Application or Activity	Technological Advance	Unit Impact	Quality of Life Impact
Systems Analysis and Systems Synthesis (design) (Operations Research and Systems Engineering)	applied mathematics + physics + systems engineering + computer simulation = system optimizations	more efficient system component and sub-system designs, new systems capabilities	+ efficiency, resulting in reduced consumptions of material and human resoures − pressures for centralized controls to avoid sub-optimizations, yielding less freedom and diversity
Economic and Industry Planning and Forecasting (Economics)	Macroeconomic theory + national income accounts data bases + computer simulations = econometric modeling	reduced industrial and national economic instability	+ job security, econometric stability − economic controls reduce freedom and diversity of choice for some
Government Policy and Program Development (Political Science)	Survey Research + sampling theory + behavioral sciences + phone and mail data gathering + computer processing = opinion, user needs, and decision modeling	social and economic problem-responsive programs development	+ responsiveness of governments policies and programs to people's needs (Security with diversity) − manipulation of public opinion to maintain political power (loss of freedom)
Organizational Development (Social Psychology)	industrial psychology + small group and individual psychology + 'reality therapies' (sensitivity training) = group behavior modification	changed organizational behaviors	+ job improvement + self-development + mental health − risk of job insecurity − loss of privacy
Individual social, emotional and cognitive development (psychology and psychiatry)	developmental psychology + psychometrics + psychoanalysis + chemotherapies = individual growth and therapeutic strategies	changed individual behaviors	+ mental health + physical security (reduced violent conflict and self-destructive behavior) + sociability (reduced hostility and inhibition) + self-development − privacy

lifetimes (from 40 to 60 years) not only feasible but widely available and desirable for health reasons themselves (25% increase in working life from 40 to 50 years – retirement at 75 rather than 65 – are already commonplace). The time is also clearly available in the aggregate from technologists as a group, if a sane world arms control policy and international scientific cooperation and efficient division of labour releases millions of technologists from unproductive or redundant work.

How can technologists become sensitive to the positive and negative impacts on quality of life that determine the overall impact of technology, and its potential survival and growth? First it is necessary to understand the quality of life concept itself, its objective components, and some ways it can be scientifically detected and measured. If quality of life can be measured, then differential technological impacts on it can be experimentally determined, and we are able to plan the application of technology in the most socially constructive way.

Table C lists some obvious and less obvious qualities of life, with associated possible indexes.

Quality of Life – What is it?

Quality of life is the characteristic that makes life desirable. It is a concept related to happiness by the implicit assumption that the one goes with the other, at least for non-masochists. It suggests there are objective, widely shared criteria for life quality, and indeed we will approach the concept in that way.

Quality of life consists of the component aspects of life that are valued. „Standard of living" no longer suffices, because many persons in nations affording a relatively high and increasing standard of living, in terms of per capita national income or GNP, believe that the overall quality of their lives as a group has nevertheless deteriorated. An example would be the middle class professional who earns more income than ever before, yet breathes worse air, wastes more time in traffic jams, is robbed and threatened more often, is woken up at night by noise more

Table C: Qualities of Life and Indexes

OBVIOUS QUALITIES OF LIFE	POSSIBLE INDEXES
Aesthetic satisfaction – perceived beauty in the look, sound, smell, feel, and taste of things	opinion poll
Quiet	(db above mean library ambient)$^{-1}$
Privacy	% of time desired visual and audio privacy is achieved
Freedom and Diversity of Choices	number of free choices / number of different choices
Sociability – 'Gemütlichkeit'	opinion poll and projective tests
Health	mean mortality, (days away from work)$^{-1}$
Entertainment	audience surveys of reactions
Physical Safety and Security	(accident and crime rate)$^{-1}$
Employment Security	(unemployment)$^{-1}$
Interesting and Rewarding Work	job advancements / job changes
Opportunities for life-long education and self-development	voluntary career changes / number of available careers, adult education enrollment
MORE SUBTLE QUALITIES OF LIFE	
A certain minimum predictability of things	(rates of change of key planning variables)$^{-1}$
Only a limited amount of frustration and difficulty in making arrangements	inverse of telephone, travel, and hotel error rates
Basic confidence in the good will and decency, or at least neutrality, of most strangers	(crime rates of non-family crimes)$^{-1}$

frequently, finds his work more repetitive than before, his children offered less through education, his neighborhood made ugly by commercial signs, and his favourite entertainments crowded out by cheap and superficial trash on television.

From an *economist's* point of view, the components of quality of life are those apsects that are scare, costly, and in demand: freedom amid diverse choices (liquidity of financial and human resources), monotony of consumption, and high preference returns on investments of effort.

From a *sociologist's* perspective, quality of life might be expressed in terms of preferred social relations: privacy when wanted, congeniality of proximate peers, role and class mobility in harmony with one's own and others' preferences and security.

From a *psychologist's* viewpoint, quality of life might consist of opportunities for satisfying self-development, rich in emotion and fantasy, yet able to deal with reality in ways effective in yielding further satisfactions; unafraid of obsolete threats, uninhibited by anxieties, unimpelled to waste any energies on self-destructive or hostile behaviours.

An *ecologist* might view quality of life in terms of the balanced maintenance of diverse life forms, with no accidental destruction of natural forms or species.

Quality of life indicators from these disciplinary points of view might include disposable (as opposed to absolute) income for the economist, available rates of social mobility for the sociologist, low rates of interpersonal conflict or depression for the psychologist, and slow rates of ecological change for the ecologist.

Given an awareness of social needs, a retained technological expertise, and a sensitive comprehension of the quality of life impacts of technological change, what can the technological planner or decision-maker do to maximize the productive and beneficial social role of technology?

The best opportunities for action probably lie in the application of problem-solving technologies, themselves mainly the fruit of technologically based industry and government activities. Table B shows how five of these problem-solving activities have exploited technological advances with resulting mostly positive and in some cases partly negative impacts on quality of life.

One of the potentially most fruitful applications of several of the problem-solving technologies would be development of *a technological division of labor among nations.* Currently the technological competition among nations wastes enormous resources through redundant R & D and piecemeal productions that do not fully exploit economies of scale. Why should several different nations have to produce operationally similar aircraft, space exploration vehicles, medical technology, etc.? Only for nationalistic and military security reasons that should abate with effective international agreements.

The efficient allocation of technological resources to social problems would classically be accomplished by equalizing the marginal returns from such applications. To do this, it is necessary to determine the absolute and relative return to quality of life components from alternative mixes of technological applications to social problems. Thus *methods of measuring the social efficiency of technology* and specific technological applications are needed.

I would propose as an initial and still crude measure of the social efficiency of technology, the arithmetic sum of the changes (positive and negative) of the quality of life components weighted by their relative popular preference among the population affected, divided by the sum of the costs of the technology in terms of both the equivalent economic cost (using shadow pricing) of the negative impacts on quality of life and the economic cost of the application.

This measure of the social efficiency of technology requires subordinate quantitative measures of the positive and negative changes in quality of life components in comensurate terms. These social impacts can be reduced to comensurate terms by expressing them in present economic value, discounting all future returns to the present. The economic returns may be derived by shadow pricing them, or determining what the impacted population now pays to achieve or avoid comparable social benefits and costs.

An example of the application of the social efficiency measures of technology would be in the *social audits* beginning to be used in a few corporations and educational and government institutions in the United States. Annual social audits present the social benefits and costs and social assets and liabilities of an organization in quantitative, dollar-equivalent terms[1]. The social audit concept adopts from financial accounting practice the idea that benefits are worth what is paid for them, or their costs. It is assumed that all social impacts such as health, security, freedom, environmental quality, etc. can be expressed in terms of the money the people concerned have actually paid for equivalent services or what they have paid to avoid equivalent costs.

Governments and industrial enterprises have always invested in data collection and measurements promising decision-making utility. This has led to a preference for hard or quantitative data, to the typical exclusion of social data and the neglect of the measurement of the social data and the neglect of the measurement of the social performance of organizations or technological innovations. The social effects, decisive as they might be for society's purposes, were expressed qualitatively and thus were not subject to test. This made it difficult for decision-makers to make rational resource allocation decisions, resulting in much of the present unhappiness with the social inefficiency of technology.

If social efficiency measures can be applied to proposed technological changes in the social audits of government and industrial organizations, then decision-makers will have a quantitative and rational basis for applying technology in optimal pursuit of social needs.

In conclusion, we must admit that there is some substance to the widespread and increasing public alarm over the degrading impacts of new technology on quality of life. Even if the net improvements in overall quality of life as a result of technological change are positive — as many of us still believe — there is still the very serious question of whether our technological efforts achieve the highest possible net positive impact in response to social needs. Clearly, much could be done that is not yet done.

We have tried to show that the gathering pessimism concerning the beneficent impacts — actual and potential — of technology applied to social purposes might gradually be reversed by a more efficient and socially responsive application of technology. This involves some re-education of technological planners and decision-makers concerning social needs and what social science research can tell us about their relative priority and interdependence; the maintenance of purely techno-logical skills, the development of an awareness of technological impacts on quality of life in technological decision-makers, the development of measures of the social efficiency of technology, as expressed in terms of quality of life impact, and the application of such measures of social efficiency of technology, as expressed in terms of quality of life impact, and the application of such measures of social efficiency of technology in comprehensive social audits of the social performance of government and industrial organizations employing technology.

References:

1) See descriptions in *Congressional Record* Jan. 20 (1970), *L'Usine Nouvelle,* Sept. (1971), *Business Week,* Nov. 27 (1971), and *Innovation,* Jan. (1972). See also the forthcoming book by Prof. Raymond Bauer of Harvard University.

SOCIAL OBJECTIVES AND NEW DESIRABLE TECHNOLOGIES

Francois Hetman
Directorate for Scientific Affairs, OECD
Paris, France

1. Threats of man-made systems

Man is fundamentally a changeful animal, change-loving and change-bound. Biologically and socially he is animated by an intrinsic need for self-assertion with respect to his environment and in particular society, his fellow men. This leads him to question continuously his condition in order to modify the world outside and reduce all kinds of risks that threaten his life. The history of the species is an endeavour to dominate nature and through this domination to improve society and man himself.

This seems to explain why scientific and technological change has been accepted so far as a fatality, as a result of 'autonomous forces', transcending individuals and societies and why higher knowledge was quasi-sacralized as a process depending on some supranatural illumination.

Imposing on nature human crafts, tools, cognitive and organizational concepts, made sustained economic growth possible as well as the liberation of man of main ancestral fears: hunger, scarcity and insecurity.

However, fostering technology and accepting it as always beneficial and as a kind of fatality has lead mankind to live now with multiple and terrifying threats: nuclear destruction, ecological disaster, depletion of natural resources. All this is accompanied by a permanent social disruption, a rapid erosion of values and a general feeling of frustration on the individual level.

Saying this is not to yield to a millenarian mood. The approach of the year 2000 differs from the hysteria of the year 1000 on one basic point: the threats we are living with are not an immanent punishment of the inherent damnation of man: they are all man-made.

As a consequence of the very 'success' of scientific and technological change, mankind is now faced with new risks and dangers which are man-made and for which there is no ecological or natural self-balancing system.

To avoid lethal disasters, men must come to new terms with man-made systems and devise new possibilities to bring scientific research and technological innovation under some kind of social control.

2. Technological determinism

There is a generally accepted and almost unquestioned conviction — whatever the political philosophy or doctrine — that technology is the fundamental factor of social change and that it acts with an irresistible and self-enhancing power on society.

This conviction is based on several currently admitted and transmitted views.

One is the contention that technological innovation is by definition a self-contained process. By its inner logic — which is the increase of specific performance and effectiveness — each technology creates opportunities for incessant new developments. In a sense, the innovators are just the 'revealers' of new steps on some basic trend representing an advance along a given functional capability. In their turn, the innovators are pushed by scientific discoveries which are made available through research and development activities. And scientific research is stimulated by the firmly held postulate of unrestrained search per se and for a better understanding of the world.

,,Although the burden of proof is on the innovator, the interdiction of a proposed new technology with clearly favorable first-order consequences is unlikely to receive social approbation, no matter how logical the interdiction may be shown to be. Only if the social costs and social gains, as well as the economic gains, can be added up and compared, and charges for these translated into economic terms, will the process of filtering or screening proposed new technologies be feasible. And no way has been found to do these tasks. The nearest approach — one that is in its prescientific stage of development — is the concept of 'social accounting' or 'social indicators'[1].

Another view rests on the thesis of benefit-cost optimization in general, both on the micro-economic and the macro-economic level. According to the optimization principle, the broad societal benefits of advances in technology exceed the associated costs sufficiently and in such a way to make technological growth inexorable. The benefits are shown up through historical comparisons of basic social categories such as reduction of working time, urbanization, health, hygiene, disposable income, etc. and through performance curves in the case of specific activities.

The costs may be more or less clearly shown up in all the negative indicators of our society — urban and environmental problems, technological unemployment, physical and mental health, etc. If we understood quantitatively the casual relationships between specific technological developments and social values, both positive and negative, we might overtly guide and regulate technological development so as to maximize their social benefit-cost relationship. Unfortunately, we have not as yet developed such a predictive system analysis. As a result, our society historically has arrived at acceptable technological benefit-cost balances empirically, i.e. by trial, error and subsequent corrective steps[2].

A similar view can be based on a methodological distinction between technological and societal phenomena. Technological forecasts come close to predictions inasmuch as they tend to concentrate on technological breakthroughs that are expected to happen sooner or later along some functional line and in a given direction of a specific performance; the only question being the precise time of occurence. On the contrary, societal forecasts can be only of a conjectural nature. The basic difference between the two categories of phenomena regards both the definiteness of content and the inevitability of occurence.

,,For instance, while the question of when electric power plants driven by thermonuclear fusion will come into existence is reasonably unambiguous, the same could not be said of the question of when alienation and impersonality of urban life will reach its maximum. There are two differences here. Societal terminology is not as precise as physical terminology, so that in general the circumstances under which a statement would be considered true are not as clearly determined. In addition, there is a certain inevitability about many physical developments whereas for most societal developments their occurence or nonoccurrence depends greatly on the presence or absence of human intervention. Thus the future of society, factually as well as semantically, is less determinate than the future of technological progress"[3].

3. Socio-cultural 'lag'

All these views are concordant to consider technology as a determinant force. This technological determinism is not only a prevalent philosophy but also the essential operational mode of current policies.

It is enhanced by the general belief — both among scientists and in the general public — that virtually anything within certain rational limits can eventually be attained if only resources and skills can be mobilized in sufficient quantities and organized for a sustained effort.

Most frequently, the technological determinism is opposed to the apparent inconsistency and lability of social phenomena. Such an opposition is often interpreted as an increasing incapacity of man and society to follow the pace set by the technological advance.

According to this interpretation, while technology is advancing at an increasing rate, human adaptability and social phenomena in general are stagnating if not receding.

This discrepancy ends up in provoking a feeling of frustration which contributes to further accentuate the lack of confidence in social institutions and a gloomy mood of all-sided alienation both on individual and social level.

Such a thinking, based either on humanistic tradition or on ideological technophoby reinforces unintentedly the thesis of technological determinism. It accepts as an evidence that human, social, and ethical phenomena lag behind technological developments[4].

In this view, social problems cannot be defined before one goes through the technology assessment. This implies that impacts are considered as being one-way, from technology to society, and that society just reacts, through feedback loops, in a rather haphazard and incongruous fashion.

Such explanations reveal a basic misinterpretation of the substance and societal role of technology. A comparison between rates of technology advance and the evolution of society is simply irrelevant. Technology is a means to social achievement — one of possible means. Its development can end up in an improvement of the means which can facilitate but not determine the social achievement. So far as technology is accepted as a fatality and proposed as an advanced milestone from which social innovation should be derived in an adaptative way, there can be no real social innovation.

Technology-triggered social innovation is a contradictory notion and a self-defeating misconception of the role of technology. It is not technology but men who are responsible for human society. The simple truth is that man as an individual does not clearly know what he would like to achieve in his life and that men as social groups do not agree on the general characteristics of society's achievement and are even unable to realize a workable consensus on a set of rules which could lead to significant social innovation.

This leads to a continuous discrediting of social institutions, their goals, their objectives and programmes. At the same time, new proposals for doing things arise. However, social innovations do not build upon the previous ones, upon an embodied experience. They come out as a result of an oscillating opposition, so that the process is essentially non-cumulative and often even regressive, for example when institutional rigidities stifle any true manifestation of new potentialities.

On the whole, the obsolescence of social innovation is probably more rapid than that of technological ones, so that there seems to be no progress but a painful groping for some sort of homeostatic equilibrium.

4. Scope of technology assessment

As a matter of fact, it is more and more obvious that technological change does not necessarily imply technological progress, real economic growth and still less an actual increase in social welfare. All criteria and the so-called measures of progress are questionned and appear to be of doubtful significance.

Hence the idea that an overall assessment of technology is of vital necessity. This idea is new insofar as it implies a conscious planning ahead of various consequences of technology and particularly of the so-called externalities, that is those aspects that have been considered till now as external to strictly technical or economic calculation. For technology to be examined from the point of view of what is socially desirable, technology assessment must be a central part of a long-range policy process striving for new social objectives and values.

Taking into account not only technological and economic, but also social, cultural, and environmental aspects means that control and management of technology is a very complex matter that will imply new relationships between science, government and industry and that will raise fundamental questions concerning the whole society and the whole social system as well as the issues of international cooperation.

The process of assessment will be difficult. For this reason, it is necessary to make a serious effort at the start in developing the methodology of technological evaluation and in constituting a large base of data with regard to directions and to the decision-making process in the field of technological developments.

Three main areas can be distinguished:

a) The first is the monitoring of negative side-effects of existing technologies and the developing of new socially more acceptable alternatives. Here one thinks quite naturally of environment and methods to abate or to avoid pollution. However, negative side-effects extend also to other fields, such as disruption of social milieu, regional and local clustering of economic power employment, professional obsolescence, migrations, haphazard urbanization, etc.

b) The second is the screening and selecting of new technologies which arise as potential developments from scientific research and already available basic knowledge.

At the present stage, this will probably be the central field of technology assessment activities. At the meeting of the Ministers of Science of the OECD, the Japanese delegation proposed in this connection that Member countries should undertake case studies and make available their experience to other Member countries. This experience would be synthetized and could thus play a role of a general warning system.

c) The third area concerns the need for new R & D in the development of new desirable technologies in relation to social goals and objectives. This supposes of course an outline of the goals of society towards which technology should be aimed at and the need for national and international mechanisms for the evaluation of the economic, social, cultural and environmental effects of particular technological options.

5. Towards the primacy of social objectives

The first two areas of technology assessment imply clearly an idea of improvement of the present situation, they tend to modify and to correct some aspects of a given state of things through an action on technology itself.

The first one deals essentially with the negative side-effects of already applied technologies, the second one involves sifting out new knowledge in order to promote new products and processes that do not present the inconveniences of the existing technologies.

These two areas of technology assessment are thus closely related to existing technologies, they are concerned essentially with the nature and the logic of each technology considered or examined. They do of course try to take into account various societal aspects but this is not primarily for the society's sake but for reorienting a given technology in a sense that can be justified on social grounds.

From the society's point of view the really innovative approach seems to be the third one. But what can be the chance of such an approach, if, as we have seen hereabove, social innovation is a self-destructing process?

There is now fatal evidence that social innovation is condemned for ever to be just a self-consuming exercise of contradicting ideologies. Undoubtedly, society is ill equipped to handle conflicting interests and to decide what kinds of technological developments could lead to the achievement of societal objectives.

Furthermore, the three categories of phenomena: a) acceleration of change, b) increasing complexity, c) simultaneous explosion and diffusion of information and stimuli makes research of possible futures and formulation of guiding societal objectives a sheer and absolute necessity.

The major problem is both the lack or inadequacy of imagination in societal innovation domains and the difficulty inherent in the fact that technology leads to social problems which are mostly recognized only when they have passed a certain critical threshold when negative aspects suddenly burst out in a quasi-cumulative way.

Without more substantial knowledge concerning the social acceptance of technological phenomena it will be hardly possible to discern social and psychological consequences of technology and still less to forecast new technologies capable of enhancing the achievement of desirable social futures.

To orient science and technology towards desirable objectives, some comprehensive view of society's goals must be elaborated to serve as a common frame of reference. This raises the problem of values: their origin, definition, contents, social and political impacts. Furthermore, present values must be confronted with nascent and discernible aspirations to adumbrate at least the area of possible future values and interests.

This raises immediately the question of how to evaluate the future desirability of a given state of affairs. Even if the values underlying current actions could .be distinctly specified, is there any chance that these values would be still operative in the future? Research of alternative futures is incomplete unless it includes the evaluation of the desirability of these alternatives.

„If we assume that this desirability is to be determined by our future rather than our present preferences ... then we have to predict our values before we can meaningfully predict our future. Or rather, since values will be affected by the future state of the world, we may face what mathematicians call a problem of iteration: we have to shift from evaluation to prediction and back to evaluation"[5].

This appears as a serious inhibition to a significant formulation of possible futures. Notwithstanding the fact that we have not an explicit and formal system of social values, it is not impossible to study the ways by which values are incorporated intrinsically into decisions. Such a systematic examination of underlying value systems may lead to a better understanding of convergent or divergent patterns of values and of reasons that push social groups to change or modify their sets of values. This also must be envisaged as a continuous process: re-evaluation and re-definition of the patterns of values will necessarily precede the formulation of alternative futures and setting of societal objectives.

6. Technology as a dependent variable

If it is admitted that technology is not an irresistible force but an element that can contribute towards societal objectives, technology can be treated as a dependent variable in the decision-making process.

The crucial problem of decision-makers is that of defining the objectives of society. This must be considered as the basic step toward a logical grouping of socio-economic programmes and subsequent technological needs.

It is impossible to avoid an explicit treatment of social goals both as to a sufficient precision and operationality of objectives which are to be defined if some action is to be undertaken. This links technology assessment techniques to methods of specifying social objectives.

From the start, objectives must be distinguished from aims, goals and wants. We consider as objectives desirable issues that are politically defendable, economically supportable and technically feasible, whereas aims and goals can be of a merely qualitative nature and can be outlined or presented out of relation to their potential resources.

The establishment of society's objectives is a function of the political process. This is particularly complex in a democracy. Let us mention just three major difficulties:

a) To define any set of viable operational objectives a large consensus is needed. This raises the basic question: who is entitled to define the objectives, in the name of which proportion and categories of population and for whom?

b) Society is continuously changing, so that the challenge of new issues makes the choice of relevant objectives particularly hard to achieve and still more to express in a meaningful way.

c) To define objectives, it is necessary to separate them from means. However, there is a strong interdependence between ends and means[6]. New means create new objectives which may again require new means and this in an asymmetric feedback way. Deciding upon the objectives without taking into account appropriate means often becomes quite arbitrary.

More fundamental difficulties arise as decision-makers try to establish not only a logical link between various objectives but also an operational modus vivendi between various levels of decision-making and a minimum of coordination between various means.

If one admits that any change in available knowledge is not necessarily a good reason for developing a corresponding technology, it is obvious that results of R & D activities should be screened and sifted through criteria of social utility. Some degree of consensus as to these criteria must be realized at all levels of social organization.

Government is supposed to take the initiative but it will be unable to act effectively unless it can bring the objectives of various levels of decision-making to at least a minimal common denominator. This may be achieved by an appropriate action on means. „The objectives of heightened sensitivity in technology assessment should, whenever possible, be achieved by structuring the incentives of individual decision-makers so that they are induced to alter their cost-benefit calculations to encompass wider concerns than have heretofore been given consideration[7].

However, this does not resolve the problem of the general understanding of all objectives through the whole social body and of their articulation on different levels of the decision-making process.

7. Programming by objectives

Science produces knowledge, that is seeds of change. These can be diffused without any apparent purpose: this can be considered as 'wild innovation'. Nowadays, organized research links them to the wish to exploit all results which can be termed as 'intensively pushed innovation'. Can it be pushed in the sense agreed on by major segments of society?

We have seen that it is not enough to define options of desirable futures. Social consensus both on objectives and means is probably still far more important. At any rate, formulating objectives seems easier than presenting them in operational terms. Operational objectives imply the need for a scale of priorities and repartition of tasks.

The first role of social innovation is to illuminate the path of technological innovation. The awareness of rapidly growing social costs related to the present pursuit of 'economic growth' suggests that it is henceforth impossible not to take into account social benefits and social costs of each single activity. All organizations must accept a social responsibility in innovation and in technological change. In the future, their vitality will depend less on the ownership of production facilities than on an efficient mix of competences and skills in the perspective of their specific contribution to priority objectives of society.

This implies that desired social innovation will have to precede technological change. Social innovation becomes then the fundamental subject matter of policy, and policy bears on finding criteria for significant desirable innovation and its role in the achievement of social objectives.

Programming by objectives consists in replacing the concept of sequence by that of a system. A system is conceived as a teleological construct which defines first of all the characteristics of a desired objective — that is to say, the desired result — and deducts from it, step by step, missions, tasks and concrete actions in the framework of a logical whole.

The scheme of programming by objectives in the field of technology shows the dependence of technological objectives on impulses coming from other categories of objectives which are supposed to be synthetized and translated into social and welfare objectives by government or other forms of consensus (Table 1).

As they get defined, technological objectives can be grouped by vectors of functional capabilities. Once the respective vector is identified and the level of possible approach ascertained, all existing technologies are explored in detail in order to obtain an appropriate picture of their characteristics. This picture is confronted with new requirements taking into account all categories of constraints (political, social, cultural, environmental, economic, technical). It leads to a general outline of a desired new technology. Such an outline is then scrutinized in a matrix of supports and resistances where all possible effects of a new technology are compared with its possible benefits. This comparison may show political or social inacceptability of the desired new technology, it may call forth new alternatives or a mere modification of existing technologies. When the need for a new technology is completely elucidated, all possible alternative methods of investigation are defined. Once the basic

Table 1: Programming by objectives in the Field of Technology

Technological objectives

Vector of functional capability

Level of relevant approach

Analysis of existing technologies

Determination of needs for new technology

Outline of desired new technology

Matrix of supports and resistances

Definition of alternative methods

Selection of basic strategy

Programme of R & D

Allocation of resources

Power objectives

Welfare and social objectives

Achievement objectives

Management objectives

strategy is chosen a suitable programme of research and development is established and resource requirements are specified.

Several feedback lines lead from the R & D programme back to the matrix of supports and resistances, to the vector of functional capability and to technological objectives to make sure that research is in line with general objectives. On the other hand, another feedback line leads to the cluster of society's objectives in order to ascertain the availability of resources in compliance with these objectives.

8. Vector of functional capability

The distinction between research-intensive or science-based sectors and research-non-intensive ones is of little use for analysis of R & D processes in relation to the development of desirable new technologies. As a matter of fact, a large part of the efforts devoted to exploration of desirable new technologies bears precisely on science-neglected sectors and on possibilities of bringing in a deep transformation of the production processes.

If a better understanding is to be reached, it is important to know how technologies co-exist, how new technologies are born and diffused. The most suitable method seems to be the 'functional capability approach' (Table 2).

Society can be represented as an array of definite functions (nutrition, lighting, housing, medical care, educational training, defence, etc., etc.). Each function is performed within a vector of functional capability which contains all technologies contributing to the performance of the function.

Each vector of functional capability can be thought of as passing through several levels of decision-making. These levels can be identified — from the most general to the most specific or from the most abstract to the most concrete — as goals of society, objectives, missions, programmes, tasks and tools (technologies).

Table 2: Vectors of Functional Capabilities

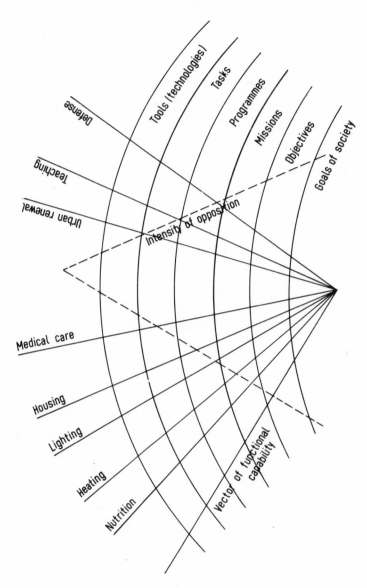

The most troublesome problem in decision-making is to find a workable linkage between all these (only logically successive) levels which implies getting fundamental ideas and concepts embodied into actions and finally into new technologies.

The difficulty of achieving consensus seems to be inversely proportional to the generality of the purpose. It is easier to get things changed at the top of the 'cone representing the intensity of opposition' than at the bottom of the level of society's goals.

This explains why, until recently, technologies have been accepted in bulk, without contention, and have become determining forces of social change.

As an example of a vector of functional capability, we can take the urban life. This will undoubtedly be one of the most acute problems of future society. If populations are not to stifle in a small number of unbearable metropoles, it is high time to think of replanning national territory if not the entire globe. Three main criteria should be taken into account: insure enjoyable healthy housing, find a stimulating symbiosis between the production function and the cultural function of the city, create new urban systems in order to restore basic ecological exchange cycles.

Incorporating these three criteria into 'general rules of housing', the government can implement an appropriate programme of technology development, inviting all interested parties, such as research institutes, university institutes, enterprises, governmental agencies, to submit projects in the form of special bids taking into account all discernible social and economic benefits and costs. The public decision-maker will then be in a position to concentrate on major strategic socio-economic issues and on dynamic criteria so as to improve and refine the quality of their choice.

9. Indicators of needs for a new technology

To identify needs for a new technology, the first step is a thorough analysis of existing technologies. After an inventory of all existing technologies within a given vector of functional capability, each technology is submitted to a general 'test of inadequacy' (Table 3).

Criteria of inadequacy are established in concordance with new technological objectives obtained by screening impulses from other categories of objectives. They are grouped in six major categories: political, social, cultural, environmental, economic and technical. Each category can be given a certain weight and within each category an internal set of weights can be adopted. Weights can be expressed as degrees of adequacy or inadequacy so that a general indicator of inadequacy can be computed for all existing technologies, allowing for a comparison between them.

The test of inadequacy can show the necessity of investigations in new directions but also some possibilities of improving existing technologies in the light of changed social and technological objectives. Existing technologies can thus be 'rejuvenated' by a limited input of new knowledge and additional technological development.

10. Profile of desired new technology

After the examination of existing technologies, their main inadequacies may serve as a starting point of investigations of the profile of the desired new technology (Table 4).

As major gaps are identified between the desired functional capability and the existing technologies, they suggest the purpose and directions of possible search.

This analysis also permits basic characteristics of desired new technology to be identified from the research and development point of view. These characteristics with their research requirements are then confronted with requirements stemming from all categories of objectives — technical, economic, environmental, cultural, social and political. This can be envisioned as a reverse to the process of determining the vector of functional capability, as one tries to start with a set of definite attributes of desired new technology and goes on comparing them with wider and more abstract concepts and objectives.

Table 3: Indicators of needs for a new technology

Criteria of inadequacy	Existing technologies				
	Technology a 1	Technology a 2	Technology a 3	Technology a 4	Technology a n
Political					
Social					
Cultural					
Environmental					
Economic					
Technical					
General indicator of inadequacy					

A = vector of Functional Capacity

Table 4: Profile of desired new technology

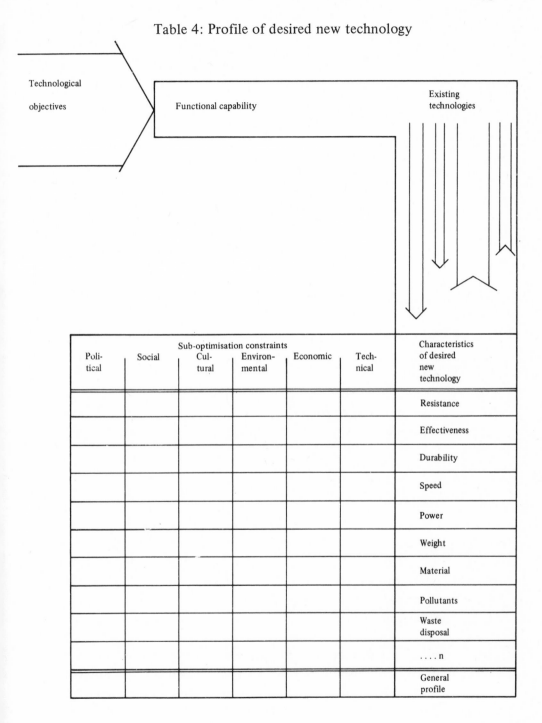

		Sub-optimisation constraints				Characteristics of desired new technology
Poli-tical	Social	Cul-tural	Environ-mental	Economic	Tech-nical	
						Resistance
						Effectiveness
						Durability
						Speed
						Power
						Weight
						Material
						Pollutants
						Waste disposal
						.... n
						General profile

For this reason, confronting the characteristics of desired new technology with requirements stemming from other objectives and issues is
considered as a sub-optimization process in which each category of
constraints tends to present the best possible rather than the optimal state
of affairs.

11. Matrix of supports and resistances

To use the programming by objective it is necessary to have a better
understanding of behavioural relations between various forces in society.
This requires a deep analysis not only of first consequences of contem-
plated new technologies but also of secondary and tertiary effects,
which means a practically continuous process of assessment of technologies within a given vector of functional capability.

In the methodological approach of the Office of Science and Technology
and The Mitre Corporation, six major categories of impacts are
distinguished[8]:
a) values and goals; b) environment; c) demography; d) economics; e)
social factors and f) institutional factors. These are further broken down
into sub-categories and may be still further divided into more detailed
classes (Table 5).

Ideally, such an impact analysis is dynamic and iterative in the sense
that it should be performed throughout the period of assessment. The
feedback loops are important as they link together the different levels
of impacts and suggest the cause-effect relationships. However, the
number of possible relationships grows rapidly with the number of
impacts. Only the largest and the most sensitive ones can possibly and
usefully be considered and examined in detail, and this is particularly true
for higher order impacts.

Before initiating research work in the field of desired new technologies,
it seems particularly useful to assess all relevant categories of discernible
benefits and costs. This can best be done within the framework of a
matrix of supports and resistances (Table 6).

Table 5: Major impact categories (From Ref. 8)

Categories	Types*
Values & Goals	Personal Community National Other
Environment	Air Water Open Space Quiet (Noise) Olfactory Weather Sunlight
Demography	Total Major Segments Rates**
Economics	Production Income Employment Prices Trained Manpower Natural Resources Inventory
Social Factors***	National Security Economic Growth Opportunity (Class Relations, Poverty) Health Education Safety (e.g., Crime) Transportation Leisure-Recreation Other Amenities
Institutional Factors	Political Legal Administrative Organization Custom-Tradition Religious

* For further subdivisions, see Reference 8.
** Migration, population density, birth and death rates, etc.
*** Goals and problems.

This matrix can be illustrated here only in its simplest form. In practice, it will undoubtedly be one of the most demanding exercises as it is supposed to take into account all groups of people concerned, each group defending fiercely its vested interests and its objectives at all levels of decision-making.

12. The 'Innovative power'

The concern with technology, its impact on man and society and the supposed socio-cultural 'lag' show clearly that from now on man cannot escape the full responsibility for his existence both as an individual and a member of society. Consequently, the concept of growth should be applied primarily to man himself, to the increase of his knowledge, skills and competences. Rather than to dominate nature, it is more important to give a really human significance to the development of man.

This presupposes that men are able to find an adequate answer to the overwhelming challenge of the increasingly complex social problems. Application of system thinking to socio-economic problems seems to be dictated by the magnitude, complexity and multiplicity of interrelationships between phenomena with respect to which empirical or intuitive methods appear not only as crude and inoperative but also too costly.

Not continuity but change is the central factor in social development. This leads to an important consequence though particularly difficult to admit: the prospect of change limits the possibilities of scientific forecasts analogous to previsional experiments in natural sciences.

This is another reason for using programming by objectives as a rolling investigation of the state of society. Its basic purpose is to contribute to the choice of a set of values on the basis of which societal priorities can be selected and lead to formulation of corresponding objectives.

This may sound presumptuous. It is impossible to take into account all factors and all interrelationships between factors. At each level, only some significant and strategic variables must be chosen if the model is to be kept operational.

Table 6: Project of a new technology matrix of supports and resistances

Resistance \ Support	Primary effects	Secondary effects	Tertiary effects	Alleged advantages of existing technologies	Suggested modifications of existing technologies
Primary benefits					
Secondary benefits					
Tertiary benefits					
Alleged benefits of general nature					
Suggested alternatives to desired new technology					

This research of desirable variants of futures can be envisaged as a continuous process of confronting values of continuity and values of change within all major social spheres. Schematically, social spheres can be represented in a sequential unending pattern which implies of course numerous and partly unknown system links and interrelationships (Table 7).

The logical thread of the projective loop is the concept of continuity. It starts with a set of existing values and steps progressively to research, education, technology, production and passes then to distribution and social, cultural and political adjustments.

On the contrary, the prospective loop starts with new sets of desirable objectives which differ from the existing set of values. These objectives are expressed as demands of political and cultural change, need for new utility functions, a different structure of production, requirements of new technologies, needs for other forms of education and for new scientific theories.

Frequently, the notion of system is confounded with the concept of auto-regulation as used in cybernetics. However, social systems do not obey to simple homeostatic principles. They advance through progressive resolution of tensions which involves the appearance of discontinuous loops and asymmetric feedback impulses.

In the last analysis, the auto-regulation principle may be considered as a modern interpretation of the classical concept of 'invisible hand'. This cannot bring a satisfying solution to many social problems which are characterized by variables of intermittent intensity and irregular or explosive feedback loops.

Complex social problems cannot be handled without some reasonable degree of visibility. Neither the fallacious quietude of cybernetic auto-regulation nor the rigidifying blinkers of authoritarian state planning correspond to basic requirements of complex social systems.

As suggested hereabove, programming by objectives seems to be a suitable framework for a goal-oriented society. Programming by objectives

Table 7: Prospective and projective loops
in the societal system

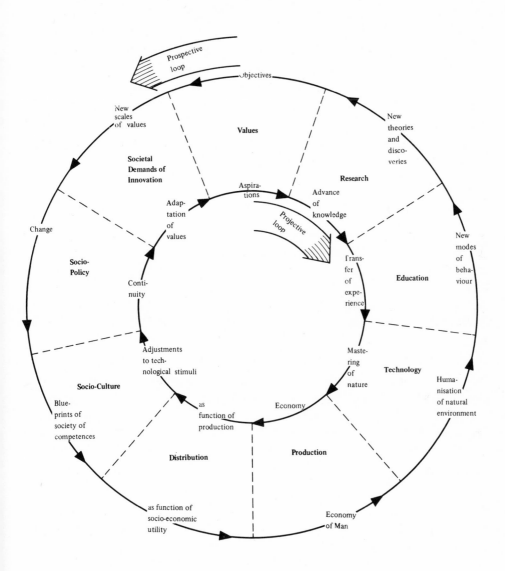

Prospective loop

Objectives

New scales of values

Values

New theories and discoveries

Societal Demands of Innovation

Research

Aspirations

Advance of knowledge

Adaptation of values

Projective loop

Change

Transfer of experience

Socio-Policy

New modes of behaviour

Education

Continuity

Adjustments to technological stimuli

Mastering of nature

Technology

Socio-Culture

Humanisation of natural environment

Blueprints of society of competences

as function of production

Economy

Distribution

Production

as function of socio-economic utility

Economy of Man

is not an attempt to reconcile vested interests but to propose new possible futures different from the past. It implies an incessant study of social processes, their sources and foci of change as well as possible consequences. It calls forth new creative tensions and questions both the existing institutions and the behavioural attitudes. It forces both the 'invisible hand' and the authoritarian planner to disclose their socioeconomic accounting to make all hands visible in order to evaluate their respective utility.

This involves the desirability of an 'innovative power' having an autonomous status in the general organization of political powers as have the three — legislative, executive and judiciary. Its main responsibility would be to explore, conceptualize and derive desirable alternative futures.

In a society of change, the essential political function is that of innovation. This implies that the three classical components of political power should be preceded by an innovative power proposing alternative societal futures. This innovative power would be institutionalized only as a framework and not as another permanent administrative body. As it is expected to foster the pluralism of initiatives, it should have a pluralistic character: for each of the great societal objectives, it could secure the cooperation of knowledgeable experts and organizations to explore the advantages and the disbenefits of each alternative, to determine the cost, and to expose as clearly as possible the expected consequences for society.

A 'national council for innovation' could be instituted to make a synthesis and present thoroughly elaborated alternative futures to the decision-makers and the public in large. The political parties would have to define their attitude in exhaustively specified programmes and socially accountable terms.

The innovative power is a condition for the programming by objective to be effective and take into account that which is central for the decision-making process: deal with phenomena of discontinuity. Programming by objectives involves, as its basic task, a continuous study of possible scientific and technological breakthroughs. However, its primary mission, on which it will be judged, is to discern social break-throughs, in other words revolts against the fossilised forms of the 'establishment' and social relationships.

The most demanding function of the innovative power would be to arbitrate between obsolescence and innovation, to discern discont-inuities, to prepare society for qualitative jumps and to define new objectives in such a way as to break factual or behavioural rigidities and to forestall ideological fanatisms.

References:

1) Franklin P. Huddle, The Social Function of Technology Assessment, in ,,Technolo-gy Assessment", Praeger, New York (1972) p. 159.

2) Chauncey Starr, Technology Assessment I—Weighing the Benefits and Risks of New Technologies? , Research Management Nov. (1970) p. 410.

3) Raul de Brigard and Olaf Helmer, Some Potential Societal Developments 1970 – 2000, Report R-7, Institute for the Future, April (1970) p. 2–3.

4) Irene Taviss, Futurology and the Problem of Values, Harvard University Program on Technology and Society, Reprint Number 12 (1969)

5) Fred Charles Ikle, Can Social Predictions Be Evaluated? Daedalus 96, Summer (1967) p. 747.

6) Charles L. Schultze, The Politics and Economics of Public Spending. The Brookings Institution, Washington (1968).

7) Technology: Process of Assessment and Choice, U. S. House of Representatives, July (1969)

8) A Technology Assessment Methodology, Some Basic Propositions, The Mitre Cor-poration, Washington, July (1971)

TECHNOLOGY ASSESSMENT – THE STATE OF THE ART

Dieter Schumacher
SYSTEMPLAN e.V.
Institut für Umweltforschung und Entwicklungsplanung
Heidelberg, Federal Republic of Germany

1. Introduction

Technology – in the context of technology assessment – has been defined as the 'systematic, purposeful application of knowledge, skill and expertise toward a function or service useful to man'[1].

Technology assessment is considered the 'thorough and balanced analysis of all significant primary, secondary, indirect, and delayed consequences or impacts, present and foreseen, of a technological innovation on society, the environment or the economy'[1].

These two admittedly broad and abstract definitions delineate an attempt to bridge the gap and harmonize the conflict between technological development on the one hand and social development (in terms of increasing what is referred to as quality of life) on the other hand.

Technology assessment is not an entirely new issue, process or method. In fact, all scientific research and development encompasses a certain assessment. However, these assessments derive their scope and value systems from a micro-world specific to the very science or technology they are being applied to. They do not extend beyond the scientific or technological subsystem of operations, whereas *social* development and consequences are left out of consideration.

The more recent and actual 'technology assessment movement' originated back in 1966, when this term first appeared in a Report of the United States Congress, House Subcommittee on Science, Research and Development, in which the threaths of potential dangerous side effects of technology were outlined[2]. Representative E.Q. Daddario subsequently introduced a bill proposing the creation of a Technology Assessment Board, claiming that 'technology assessment is a form of policy research which provides a balanced appraisal to the policy maker. Ideally, it is a system to ask the right question and obtain correct and timely answers. It identifies policy issues, assesses the impact of alternative courses of action and presents findings. .... The focus of technology assessment will be on those consequences that can be predicted with a useful degree of probability [3].

Six years later, the Technology Assessment Act of 1972 was signed by the President of the United States[4], establishing an Office of Technology Assessment, a Technology Assessment Board and Advisory Council, and designing the impact of the Act on the services of the Library of Congress, the General Accounting Office, and the National Science Foundation. The first annual budgets of the Office have been set at a level of $ 5 000 000 per year.

The following paper attempts to review the present state of this movement, in particular with respect to the applicability to *other* countries, to the objectives of technology assessment, to potential subjects and issues, to suitable methodological approaches, and — last but not least — to appropriate institutional arrangements and the constraints involved.

2. Objectives of Technology Assessment

For a number of reasons, it is not surprising that the United States has been and still is the spearhead of the technology assessment movement. Historically, its launching coincides with the following phenomena, emerging rather early and with particular intensity (with respect to other countries) in the United States.

- A public disenchantment with respect to technologies (either new or obsolete old ones), deploring the problems created by technologies and calling for a 'technology stop'.

- More specifically, the environmental issue and the related public awareness and sensitivity.

- The pile-up of technologies and technological prototypes developed during the 'technology boom' in the 1960ies and only scarcely transferred into real innovations.

- An increasing discrepancy between technological skills and potential on the one hand and the impact of technological solutions on complex social system problems on the other hand.

- As a consequence, a lack of 'convincing' goals for national and international technology policies.

- An increasing desire and need to rationalize public administration operations and to improve performance by providing analytical tools.

- An increasing pressure on public funding of technology programmes because of rising costs and claims and limited resources.

Technology assessment has been and still is considered a useful tool to cope with all these challenges. By careful application of assessment processes, one hopes

- to introduce new and more convincing (rational) elements into technology policy making,

- to develop—by means of such policy — more useful and less harmful technologies,

- to develop technologies which provide significant contributions to solving public and social problems,

It is important to emphasize that technology assessment is not or should not be a notion and committment of government and public administration only. On the contrary, it has a bearance on all parties, institutions and individuals who are involved in the process of technology development. Technology assessment means a new way of looking at technologies, attempting to transfer technology from the status of an independent variable of social change into a dependent determinant, which in turn corresponds to a shift from isolated to comprehensive technology planning. This clearly is a joint responsibility of government, of the science community, of industry, and of individual researchers, of planners, and of those engaged in product development and marketing services. If the development of technologies were cancelled because of the problems they caused, the world would not become any better. In fact, there is no alternative to the continued use and development of technologies. Therefore, technology assessment is a predominant tool and challenge for those who want to contribute to the improvement of our living conditions.

Furthermore, one should emphasize that technology assessment, by its very nature, is not a tool of big science or advanced technology development only. It is true that so far the majority of full size technology assessment analyses (see below) ran at a level of effort that can be afforded for the purposes of big national issues and decisions only. From a philosophic point of view, however, technology assessment applies just as well or even more closely to every day technologies, solving problems which originate from our daily life and experience. The latter notion is in line with new guidelines for science and technology policy making[5) 6)].

Thus, the objectives of technology assessment are briefly

— to make better use (in a quality-of-life- and public-acceptance - sense) of present or future technologies, and, to that end,

— to improve the planning, programming and budgeting operations in technology development.

While these objectives are rather general and a challenge to government, science, industry and individuals, the United States have so far focussed their technology assessment activities predominantly on the public policy sector. The Congressional records describe technology assessment as a way of 'equipping Congress with new and effective means for securing competent, unbiased information concerning the physical, biological, economic, social and political effects of technology applications; and utilize this information whenever appropriate, as one factor in the legislative assessment of matters pending before the Congress'[7)].

A further reduction of scope has occured in the United States in that the majority of assessments performed so far have been dealing with economic and environmental impact analysis. Quite a few potential and rewarding fields of applying technology assessments have not yet been covered by in depth studies. We are only at a beginning. It is needless to say that in other countries the overall level of efforts and (therefore) perhaps even the objectives of technology assessment are somewhat different from those observed in the United States[8)9)].

Speaking in more operational terms and leaving to some extent the above-mentioned *general* level of understanding, technology assessment is dealing with a total cost / total benefit analysis of technological developments, where

Total Cost = Direct Cost + Indirect Cost (i.e. undesirable side-effects)
and
Total Benefit = Direct Benefit + Indirect Benefit (i.e. desirable side effects).

According to G. Strasser[10)], technology assessment is 'a systematic planning and forecasting process that delineates options and costs, encompassing economic as well as environmental and social considerations, that are both external and internal to the programme or product in question, with special focus on technology-related bad as well as good effects'.

Even more frankly speaking, G. Strasser described technology assessment as (classical) systems engineering + more diffused program-me (product) objectives + more contributing disciplines + emphasis on side effects[10)].

As will be outlined below in more detail, this operational level involves a large amount of critical bottlenecks, centered around the problem of describing and quantifying social phenomena and elements of quality of life [11)] and relating these to technology and to the classical programme or product accounting systems. Putting (widely accepted) values to technological developments and their impacts is one of the prime and most crucial objectives of technology assessment. We do know very much about these social systems, but we cannot (yet) measure their components. Social indicators would be useful, but should be employed with precaution. The fascination of having a rather managable analytical technology assessment tool should not induce us to oversimplify the pluralistic scenario of our society [12] [13].

In view of these difficulties and of past experiences, one should aim at an optimum mix of securing the high level challenges and objectives of technology assessment and at the same time adopting a rather modest and pragmatic approach to the assessment issue. Sophisticated complex models are often achieved at the expense of practicability and applicability only, and would therefore not be of any use.

3. Technology Assessment Subjects and Issues

Potential subjects and issues for an assessment analysis are in principle all impact areas of technologies. Institutionally speaking, this means that — in principle — all organizations and organizational units dealing with technology applications could (should) have an interest in assessment processes.

In general, technology assessment may be applied to

- *macrosystems,* such as energy supply, urban mass transportation, supersonic transport, etc., as well as to
- *microsystems* (components), such as high strength materials, fire protection equipment, machine tools, artifical organs, etc.

The former, *big* assessments usually involve major public policy issues or problems of urban, regional, national or international importance. They, therefore, require a strong government committment in providing for suitable assessment organizations, manpower and resources. The latter, *small* scale assessments may be located on a level of relevance corresponding to individual laboratories and industrial companies or to certain industries and branches. They are less voluminous in scope and budget and may (should) be performed predominantly under private initiative.

Any assessment organization or team should develop a list of selection *criteria* for suitable subjects and issues, in order to limit and structure to some extent the demands for assessments being forwarded to it. As an example, the following list has been established for the United States Technology Assessment Board [14]:

(1) Criteria intrinsic to *the issue:*

   a) Scope of impacts

   b) Irreversibility of consequences (denying society future freedom of choice)

   c) Severity of impacts

   d) Feasibility of Congressional action.

(2) Criteria as to *the way the issue is regarded:*

   a) Evidence of prospective public concern − importance and urgency likely to be attached to it by the public

   b) Estimated importance and urgency as judged by a requesting Congressional committee

   c) Relationship of the subject to ongoing investigations by Congressional committees

   d) Relationship of the subject to studies being conducted by or for the executive branch.

(3) Criteria concerning the compatibility of a proposed assessment with *resources available:*

   a) Availability of an organization (or several organizations) competent to perform assessment functions in the subject area

   b) Funds available

   c) Ability of the Office of Technology Assessment staff to process the assignment by preparing a work statement, terms of reference, and other elements of a Request for Proposal

   d) Availability of information sufficient to make the assessment.

For *industrial* assessment functions and issues, a similar set of criteria would be readily available.

As far as technology and public policy is concerned, V. T. Coates has prepared a rather detailed analysis of assessment activities going on in some 86 offices in executive agencies of the United States Federal Government [15]. From 97 exemplary studies collected, the bulk was concerned with environmental issues or focussed on specific societal problems to which technology would seem to be a contributor to possible solutions.

The full impact and context of technology assessment for public administration, scientific and industrial action is best demonstrated by a list of issues raised or referred to during the Congressional debates on assessment in the United States [16]. Since this list is (a) illustrative and (b) not widely distributed, it is included in part in the Appendix.

It is needless to say that not a single office or institution could have a responsibility and competence to deal with all these issues. The list demonstrates, however, to what extent technology assessment activities penetrate practically all branches of policy making, scientific progress, industrial development and production, and − last but not least − the quality of life.

4. Methodological Approaches to Technology Assessment

As has been outlined before, technology assessment is a *process,* a vital part of development planning in all fields of social development, as far as a relevance to technology or to an impact of technology exists. Methodologies are thus trying to *organize* this process and to subdivide it into specific operational steps. A list of some 30 references dealing with methodologies has been prepared by G. J. Knezo [17].

Generally speaking, there are two basic ways of dealing with a given issue: The *case study approach* and the *model building approach* [10].

When working in terms of *case studies,* the assessment team generally operates very closely to the real world: The assessment analysis attains a high degree of relevancy and practicability. Employing standard systems analysis techniques, the team usually succeeds in drawing up all essential elements in the issue and designs a strategy of how to approach the solution planning. This straight-forwardness and pragmatism is feasible at the expense of the transferability of the results to similar issues in other problem environments.

The model building approach, on the other hand, attempts to develop a rather general model description of the issue, transferable to other problem environments, with a tendency of being abstract and only partially applicable to real problems. There is the danger of sticking to data which fit into the model rather than describing reality.

This methodological dilemma between the two approaches can, of course, be avoided by applying a mix of both in an iterative fashion, if the resources do allow for such effort.

A special kind of case study approach is that of *comparative analysis,* which is of particular interest for evaluating assessment studies performed in different countries or by different analysts.

Perhaps the most detailed break-down into individual *assessment process phases* has been elaborated by the Mitre Corporation[18]. Since the seven steps designed by the MITRE team have become a standard approach, they will be briefly reproduced and illustrated here (from reference 18):

Step 1: *Define the assessment task*

using categories like range of technologies, range of topics, groups affected, time period analyzed, types and levels of impacts, impact measurements, etc.

Step 2: *Describe relevant technologies*

using a Technology Description Background Statement and addressing physical and functional aspects, current state of the art, influencing factors, related technologies, future state of the art, uses and applications, etc.

Step 3: *Develop state of society assumptions*
addressing categories like values, environment, demography, economic and social institutions, etc.

Step 4: *Identify impact areas*
using categories like in step 3.

Step 5: *Make preliminary impact analysis*
by preparing a key impact comparison with and without action options, and using impact characteristics like affected groups, nature of effect, likelihood, timing, magnitude, duration, diffusion, source, controllability, etc.

Step 6: *Identify possible action options*
using criteria like controllability, worth, priority, effectiveness, cost (sponsor), cost (spill-over), nonfinancial problems, institutional obstacles, uncertainty, etc.

Step 7: *Complete impact analysis*
along the lines of step 5.

These methodological steps were tested in the MITRE studies by application to pilot technology assessments of automotive emissions, computers-communications networks, enzymes (industrial), mariculture (sea farming), and water pollution (domestic wastes).

However sophisticated and skilled methodologies are, there is always need for pragmatism and compromise in real technology assessment tasks. A problem-oriented approach is unlikely to succeed if a classical or prefabricated methodology is applied without adaption to the particular issue. This holds in particular for the operational levels into which the above-mentioned 7 steps split up. There is no *one* methodology for technology assessment. This is seen, for example, in such operations as cost-benefit analysis or measuring a social phenomenon by indicators. For these reasons, major learning effects on how to do technology assessment should be drawn from the numerous case studies, besides looking at the more general and abstract methodology and model building papers.

5. Constraints and Consequences

This remark brings us to the question of constraints and consequences. Other than in technical domains, the analytical tools and procedures have to be redesigned practically in each individual technology assessment study. The above-mentioned 7 steps or other basic methodologies do not provide but an almost trivial (but logical) framework and guideline for the entire assessment process.

Technology assessment studies must be in depth. Superficiality bears the danger of leading to considerable negative side effects if decision making is based upon such analysis.

This involves the financial constraint in that technology assessment studies are rather expensive, in the order of several $ 100 000, at least for the above-mentioned macro-systems. However, if the latter really involve national issues, a given country should be able to afford a few studies of this nature per year. It is emphasized that usually the budget for prototype development of a given technology or product exceeds an assessment budget by several orders of magnitude. Thus, assessment efforts *before* major decision making appear to be worthwhile.

Technology assessment objects should preferably be medium size in order to achieve a resolution of the issues involved. Big systems have a tendency that everything depends on everything. As a consequence, the study is hard to split up into individual, well defined and comprehensive action options. On the other hand, systems too small in scope have a danger of leading to unit-oriented actions rather than systems-oriented ones, leaving the overall problem solving impact suboptimized. Finally, constraints naturally also arise from the organizational and institutional aspects and the particular environment, in which the assessment process is to be performed. This issue is discussed in more detail in Chapter 6 and in the papers of D. Altenpohl, H. Geschka, G. Schaude and the author in this Volume.

6. Organizational and Institutional Aspects

Technology assessment is not an isolated process or separable from the institutions responsible for and dealing with technological and social development planning. Any assessment study, which is not prepared with reference to, in the light of or for the service of particular administrations, corporates etc. are likely to have limited impact only.

Technology assessment efforts cannot and should not be superimposed on existing institutions; they must be embeded into the latter. *New* institutions created e.g. for assessment studies have a tendency of making obsolete institutions (with respect to technology development) even more obsolete. The set up of an Office of Technology Assessment (OTA) in the United States Legislative Government branch is likely to absorb responsibilities and functions which so far — to some extent — have been or should have been performed by other institutions. The OTA, therefore, may become powerful at the expense of some other part of public administration. Naturally, OTA may also become a stimulator and pace-maker for other institutions and private business. However, one should not underestimate the danger of the fascination inherent in any new institute to be installed.

It has been mentioned before that technology assessment is not a substitute for decision making; rather, it may help to arrive at more rational decisions. Nevertheless, the technical expertise involved in an assessment is hard to assess by laymen. Therefore, an assessment study is likely to have a large impact on decision making, provided that it is channelled into appropriate structures of responsibility.

This brings up the question of *neutrality* and *objectivity*. Since in no country there is a space completely free from scientific, technical, social, economic, or political pressure, it is almost impossible to guarantee and institutionalize these two virtues. There are essentially two schools of thought: Those aiming at neutrality, and those considering assessment a kind of advocacy process, where different opinions are being balanced by organized conflicts. The OTA is being held to merely analyze issues and inform Congress. It is not supposed to interfere with decision making or recommendations to political leaders. In the United Kingdom, on the other hand, the so-called Royal Commissions do have a mission including recommendations; they often extend their activities far into the decision making process.

Other countries are less advanced in setting up national technology assessment structures. In general, governments and private industry are still experimenting with various kinds of organizational frameworks. See papers of D. Altenpohl, H. Geschka, G. Schaude and the author in this Volume.

7. Conclusions and Future Tasks

Technology assessment is not as new as it is sold nowadays, but it means a challenge to all institutions and individuals active in technology development. Both product development in industry and technology programmes of governments have to be extended into these dimensions of thought and social committment.

Governments do have a clear-cut responsibility to become actively engaged in technology assessment processes. However, technology assessment is not a public task only. In fact, such narrowing would lend to the assessment movement a 'prosecuting image', comparable to the role of the Attorney General in judicial systems.

The overall benefit would be larger, if entrepreneurs themselves would assume technology assessment philosophies and operations, leading to new types of products, of markets and perhaps even of consumerism.

Technology assessment should be detached from the environmental issue. Sure, practically all technologies and products have an impact on the (physical and/or social) environment, but technology assessment is not a tool of environmental policy making only. It has a bearance and significance of its own.

The *American* way of organizing and performing technology assessment is very much linked to the environmental issue, to the legislative process and designed for the specific Congressional scene and mentality. A transfer of these modes to other countries may be difficult. In *Europe,* e.g., technology assessment is hoped and expected to include a presumably larger amount of social desirability elements, as became apparent at the NATO Advanced Study Institute on Technology Assessment (ref. 12 and 13). European governmental services and parliaments do have a general awareness of the problems and issues at stake, but lack — with respect to the United States' scene — a certain degree of pragmatism and 'learning-by-doing' -philosophy. This is why European countries have to design their own way of organizing technology assessment.

Europe should also make efforts to avoid being fragmented into several *national* assessment landscapes. It should rather strive for a crossfrontier responsibility and committment for a joint technology development. The prospects for technology assessments on a European level are, however, rather scarce, since there is no use in institutionalizing technology *assessment* without having a technology *policy* and corresponding institutions. The Roman Common Market Treaties do not provide for an administrative and political scene in which an Office-of-Technology-Assessment-type unit could be vitalized. Even if we had an OTA in Bruxelles, its impact on *national* technology policies would be negligble in view of the present deficiencies in European technology policy making.

Finally, a predominant task for the future is the synthesis of technology assessments into *technology transfer* processes, since the latter are supposed to transfer new technologies into application fields, maximizing positive impacts and side-effects. Especially technology transfer into *developing countries* needs these new lines of thought. We cannot develop sophisticated technology assessment schemes for domestic purposes and apply different (obsolete) value systems elsewhere.

Hence, the technology assessment philosophy should become a major line of thought in all issues concerned with and relevant to technology. It is a promising tool for further drawing a maximum of benefit from new and old technologies and at the same time for minimizing their negative side-effects.

References

1) Technology Assessment for the Congress, U.S. Congress, Senate, Committee on Rules and Administration, November 1 (1972), U.S. Government Printing Office, Washington (1972)

2) Science and Technology: Review and Forecast, Second Progress Report, U.S. Congress, House, Subcommittee on Science, Research and Development, 89th Congress, 2nd Session, U.S. Government Printing Office, Washington (1966) p. 25

3) Technology Assessment, Statement of Subcommittee on Science, Research and Development, 90th Congress, 1st Session, U.S. Government Printing Office, Washington (1967) p. 12-13

4) Technology Assessment Act of 1972, Public Law 92 − 484, see also ref. 1, p. 43−50

5) Toward a Science Policy for the United States, U.S. Congress, House, Subcommittee on Science, Research and Development, 91th Congress, 2nd Session, U.S. Government Printing Office, Washington, October 15 (1970)

6) Science, Growth and Society, Report of the Ad hoc Group on New Concepts of Science Policy, OECD, Paris (1971)

7) U.S. Congress, House Report 10243 (1972), p. 2−3, (Public Law 92 − 484).

8) Compare OECD Seminar on Technology Assessment, Paris, January (1972) − Mimeo Papers.

9) See D. Schumacher, this Volume

10) G. Strasser, Methodology for Technology Assessment, Experience in the United States, OECD Seminar on Technology Assessment, Paris, January (1972).

11) See G.J. Stöber, this Volume

12) H. David, NATO-Advanced Study Institute of Technology Assessment, Lake Garda, Italy, Sept. 18−29 (1972)

13) G.J. Stöber and D. Schumacher, Ibid.

14) Ref. 1, p. 51 − 52

15) V. T. Coates, Technology and Public Policy, The Process of Technology Assessment in the Federal Government, Program of Policy Studies in Science and Technology, The George Washington University, July (1972)

16) See Ref. 1, p. 79

17) G.J. Knezo, Technology Assessment Vol. 1, No. 1, (1972); see also Ref. 1, p. 83

18) A Technology Assessment Methodology, The Mitre Corporation, in cooperation with and for the Office of Science and Technology, Executive Office of the President, Washington, June (1971), see also reference 1, p. 64 – 67.

Appendix

Selected Issues Raised in Reports and Hearings on the Subject of Technology Assessment in the United States Congress (from Reference 16).

Categories. Environment, Energy, Social Action, Health and Safety, National Resources, International Issues, Miscellaneous

1. Environment Issues: Air pollution
Aircraft noise and environmental effects
Alaska pipeline
Atmospheric research
Automobile pollution
Damming of rivers
Defoliating herbicides
Detergents
DDT
Internal combustion engine alternatives
Internal combustion engine pollution
Jet aircraft noise
Lead in the atmosphere
Leaded gasoline
Location of nuclear power reactors
Long term climatic effects of atmospheric pollution
Mutagens introduced into the environment
Noise abatement and control
Noise pollution and standards
Nuclear power plant waste disposal
Offshore oil drilling and pollution
Persistent pesticides
Solid waste management
Water pollution
Weather modification

2. Energy Issues:

Breeder reactors
Civilian nuclear reactors
Energy management
Energy production and utilization
Fusion power sources
Imbalances in energy supply and demand
Natural gas shortage
Nuclear power
Power generation and transmission
Safeguards for nuclear reactors and materials

3. Social Action Issues:

Civil desorder
Community cohesion
Computers and the invasion of privacy
Crime control
Developments in the life sciences
Eperimental cities
Future quality and form of life
Highways
Housing
Human resources management and development
Job motivation
Population growth and concentration
Problems of the cities
Social and economic issues of the SST
Technology and urban development
Traffic congestion
Transportation and snarls
Urban overcrowding

4. Health and Safety Issues:

Automobile air bag
Artificial heart
Biomedical consequences of radioactivity
Birth control
Comprehensive medical care
Drugs
Food additives
Genetic engineering
Lead poisoning from paints
Public health measures
Radiation levels and exposure hazards
Thalidomide

5. Natural Resources Issues:

Natural resources development
Resources management
Unnecessary waste of natural resources

6. International Issues:

Arms control
Chemical and biological warfare
Communications satellites and technology
Earth resources satellites
Global cooling of the atmosphere
New defense equipement
Nuclear weapon fallout
Oil pollution of the high seas
The seabed

7. Other Issues:

Agricultural technology
Air traffic control
Bridge safety
Computer technology
Cybernation
Longe-range weather forecasting
Metric system
Nuclear explosions for civil purposes
Outer space
Oceanography

Social Indicators and Other Tools for Measuring Quality of Life

MEASURING THE QUALITY OF LIFE USING SAMPLE SURVEYS

John Hall
Survey Unit, Social Science Research Council
London, United Kingdom

1. Introduction

Much is written these days on measuring the state of cities and of nations by deriving social indicators from 'hard' and 'semi-hard' data in the shape of economic and social statistics. In the United States there is the work of Sheldon and Moore[1], Olson[2] and Bauer[3]. In Britain we have the new publication 'Social Trends' from the Central Statistical Office, whose Director has published an article with the actual title 'Measuring the Quality of Life'[4] The Social Science Research Councils of the U.S.A. and U.K. recently held a joint conference on Social Indicators, the proceedings of which have been published in book form[5]

The search for social indicators has now spread to the use of 'soft' data with which to fill out the social account. In conjunction with Professors Angus Campbell and Philip Converse of the University of Michigan, the Survey Unit is currently investigating the possibility of deriving new subjective indicators, more descriptive of how people actually *feel* about the quality of their lives. What is envisaged is a systematic longitudinal study of perceived satisfactions and dissatisfactions in order to pinpoint possible future problematic areas, and to measure the progress of existing attitude changes.

We hope to establish, as Campbell and Converse[6] say, a research programme devoted to the generation of information regarding the aspirations, attitudes, satisfactions, disappointments, grievances, expectations and values of the British population. For whilst objective conditions of life may, in some aspects, have changed for the 'better' in that there is less hunger, 'better' housing, 'better'schools, 'better'transport etc., there may not be an equivalent subjective change in feelings that life is also 'better'. People do not necessarily feel more secure, or more self-fulfilled.

Campbell and Converse claim somewhat tritely, but accurately, that the quality of life must be in the eye of the beholder, and it is only through an examination of the experience of life as our people perceive it that we shall understand the human meaning of the great social and institutional changes that characterize our time.

2. Formulation

After a review of available empirical literature, notably Campbell and Converse[6], Bradburn[7], Robinson [8] and Kilpatrick and Cantril[9], a series of depth interviews with members of the public, and reading essays by children on 'happiness', we were able to make hypotheses about inputs to a sense of life-satisfaction, but we are not so heavily committed to them that we cannot change them or postulate new ones. First we defined various life-areas such as health, district, job, and leisure with which people might be satisfied or not, which we called domains. Secondly, we needed to be able to discern the effects on reported satisfaction of personality syndromes and short term changes of mood. Thirdly, we included background variables such as sex, age, class, educational level and income.

This gave rise to three models to guide the investigation. The simplest model hypothesizes a measurable sense of overall life-satisfaction which is some kind of summation of satisfactions and dissatisfactions with particular aspects of life (See Fig. 1 a). Fig. 1 b introduces the concepts of positive and negative affect (after Bradburn) and hypothesizes that some domains may contribute to life-satisfaction only through positive affect, others through negative. Thirdly we postulated that reports of satisfaction with life or with life domains may in fact all be determined by some underlying social-psychological syndrome or personality factors. Each of these models should be seen in the context of the background variables.

Fig. 1a

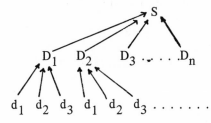

S = Generalized life-satisfaction

D = Generalized domain-satisfaction

d = Specific satisfiers and dissatisfiers.

Fig. 1b

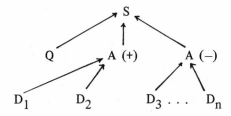

A = General Affect

Q = Other components of S.

Fig. 1c

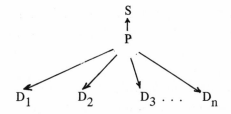

P = Personality Syndrome

Fig. 1 Models used in Investigation

3. Methodology

To date three surveys have been conducted, known respectively as

(a) Pilot I (Quota sample of 213, United Kingdom, March 1971)

(b) Pilot II (Quota sample of 593, 8 major conurbations. Oct.-Nov. 1971)

(c) Oxlife (Random sample of 173, Oxford, July 1972)

For Pilot I our basic measure of satisfaction both for domains and overall life-satisfaction was a vertical ladder-scale numbered 0-10 based on that used by Cantril[9]. To measure anomy we used the 7-item Srole scale augmented by 6 items suggested by Christie to offset response set. Indirect measures of overall life-satisfaction were items concerning a wish to change past and present lives, and distances from ideal selves.

Pilot II represented the British part of the cross national work with Campbell. For comparability the ladder scale was changed to run from 1 to 7. The indirect measures of life-satisfaction were replaced by a semantic differential scale of life-satisfaction adjectives, and the anomy scale was reduced to seven items. Some domains were dropped, new ones added, and an attempt was made to discover components of domain satisfactions by obtaining ratings on specific aspects within them.

Oxlife was a practical exercise for students attending our 1972 summer school on survey methods. It was concerned with only 5 domains, but had new items in the form of a semantic differential scale for self-assessment, and in the questions relating to goal achievement and feeling happy, which were used by Bradburn[7].

Respondents had no difficulty in using the ladder-scales to give ratings either for themselves or attributed to others. We ourselves are not quite sure exactly how people are using them and consequently face dilemmas in analysis. For instance, should we standardize on variables or on people? However, multivariate techniques offer some validation of the technique since all variable groupings produced by the analysis are consistent with sociological sense if not with common sense; some variables are regrouped in a different order to that in which they were used in the questionnaires.

One reservation we have about using these scales, before everyone rushes off to try them, is that the distributions are very heavily skewed towards the top except in those domains where blame for discontent lies other than with self. Thus these distributions may reflect a desire to keep up appearances, or they may be some kind of constant, in the sense that whatever the objective conditions of residence, work, leisure, health, the levels of satisfaction will be the same. Perhaps 'satisfied' is not the right question to ask; perhaps 'happy' or 'content' would be better. These questions can only be answered by further methodological research.

As a further check on validity, respondents were asked to rank, in order of importance for life-satisfaction, the domains for which they had given self-ratings.

4. Findings

It would be inappropriate to embark on a detailed presentation of our findings since these are available upon request direct from the Unit. I would rather like to briefly illustrate the nature of the results in the three surveys.

Pilot I

In the first few questions of Pilot I, respondents were asked to ascribe satisfaction ratings to a list of socio-economic groups and then to themselves. They were then asked to which group they themselves belonged. This gave us 3 kinds of ratings to compare (See Table 1).

1. The average rating given to each group by everyone else
2. The average rating given to each group by those who later placed themselves in the group
3. The overall self-rating on (a) present and (b) entitlement

Table 1: Average ratings of satisfaction with 'Things in general today'

Pilot I March 1971 (Scale 0–10) Ratings of	Unskilled Workers	Skilled Workers	Office Workers	Professional People	Business executives	Small businessmen	Old age Pensioners
Group by all other groups	4.36	5.64	5.86	7.26	8.05	5.02	2.44
Group by those in group	3.75	5.46	6.13	5.95	7.68	2.90	2.66
Satisfaction by those in group	4.75	5.64	6.04	5.91	6.84	4.10	4.74
Entitlement by those in group	7.10	7.45	7.74	7.86	8.32	6.40	6.91

These and other findings from Pilot I are fully discussed by Abrams and Hall [10] and will not be elaborated on here.

Table 2 shows the average self-ratings of satisfaction on each domain, the average rank position of each domain in importance for life-satisfaction, correlations between these ratings and overall life-satisfaction and anomy, and a discrepancy index to highlight areas of high importance which have high satisfaction or dissatisfaction. The correlation coefficients shown are multiplied by 100 and rounded to two places for ease of presentation.

What have we actually measured here? We suspect that reported satisfaction is largely based on perceived slice of Gross National Product. Correlational and factor analysis confirm our suspicions of an economic bias, the variables falling into three distinct clusters. Since one of these clusters apparently measured most closely what we defined as 'Quality of Life', we consequently designed the survey Pilot II to keep the overall life-satisfaction items well away from economic or any other contamination.

Table 2: Domain satisfactions and relation with overall satisfaction and anomy

Pilot I	Average rating	Rank		Index of Discrep-ancy*	Correlations	
		Satis-faction	Import-ance		Things in general	Anomy
Domains						
Family life	8.77	1	2	+ 10	+ 17	− 17
Friendships	8.09	2	7	+ 4	+ 08	− 10
Health	8.05	3	1	+ 7	+ 10	− 12
Housing	7.89	4	5	+ 3	+ 13	− 05
Job	7.83	5	4	+ 2	+ 24	+ 01
District	7.44	6	9	0	+ 03	− 11
Leisure	7.33	7	11	0	+ 24	− 18
Children's education	7.23	8	8	− 2	+ 14	− 04
Police & law-courts	6.91	9	10	− 1	− 04	− 12
Welfare Services	6.51	10	6	− 5	+ 37	− 20
Financial Situation	5.48	11	3	− 9	+ 52	− 36

(*Discrepancy index obtained by *(6 − Satisfaction Rank) x (12 − Importance Rank) ÷ 5* and rounding to nearest integer. This brings items low on importance to the centre of the scale and scores high positive for high satisfaction and high negative for high dissatisfaction on the important domains.)

100

Pilot II

Comparison of the Pilot II figures (See Table 3) shows that this strategy was justified. It is immediately apparent that each of the domains except religion taps some aspect of the dimension measured by reported satisfaction.

Table 3: Domain satisfactions and relation to overall satisfaction, semantic differential score and anomy.

Pilot II November 1971 Scale 1–7	Average rating	Rank		Index of Discrepancy	Correlations		
		Satisfaction	Importance		„Life as a Whole"	S.D. Score	Anomy
Domains							
Marriage	6.51	1	1	+ 11	+ 23	+ 37	− 09
Family Life	6.12	2	1	+ 9	+ 38	+ 36	− 20
Job	5.99	3	6	+ 4	+ 33	+ 37	− 18
District	5.74	4	7	+ 2	+ 24	+ 21	− 15
Health	5.74	4	3	+ 4	+ 24	+ 28	− 12
Spare time	5.53	6	9	0	+ 40	+ 45	− 19
House	5.43	7	5	− 1	+ 19	+ 14	− 12
Standard of Living	5.12	8	4	− 3	+ 36	+ 34	− 26
Education	4.92	9	8	− 2	+ 27	+ 13	− 10
Level of Democracy	4.67	10	11	− 1	+ 25	+ 19	− 24
Comfort from Religion	4.01	11	9	− 3	+ 05	+ 10	− 13

Cluster analysis produces one large cluster and two smaller ones. Factor analysis has shown an underlying general factor accounting for 15% of the sample variance, but it takes a further 19 factors to achieve 60%. The best linear regression we have so far produced accounts for only 37% of the variation in reported overall life-satisfaction, for the whole sample. This rises to 60% for certain sub-groups.

'Oxlife'

The value of the Oxford survey lies principally in the simultaneous use of four separate measures of general life-satisfaction, two of which were used for the first time in the United Kingdom together with anomy and a new semantic differential concerned with 'the sort of person I feel I am'. Instead of 'my present life' the heading for the life-satisfaction semantic differential was 'compared to most people I feel my life is'.

Even allowing for bias due to trainee interviewers, we were surprised to find a low correlation between the scores on this scale and the answers to the question 'taking all things together, would you say you were: very happy, fairly happy, or not too happy? '

Conclusion

The multivariate work we have done so far would seem to justify our 'life-domains' approach, but there do appear to be a large number of distinct dimensions in the data, and we have yet to find a satisfactory dependent variable from among our measures of general life-satisfaction. Our anomy variable is consistently and negatively related to almost all of the satisfaction measures, but even with this, the major part of the variation in overall satisfaction, whichever measure we take as the dependent variable, is left unaccounted for. In future the work must take account of social-psychological syndromes and mental states.

102

References:

1) E. B. Sheldon and W. E. Moore (Ed.), Indicators of Social Change Russell Sage Foundation, New York (1968)

2) M. Olson, Jun., An Analytical Framework for Social Reporting & Policy Analysis, Annals of the American Academy of Political and Social Science, March (1970)

3) R.A. Bauer, Social Indicators, Cambridge, Mass., M.I.T. Press (1966)
   Social Indicators and Sample Surveys, Public Opinion Quarterly, 30 (1966)

4) C. Moser, Measuring the Quality of Life" New Society, 10th December (1970)

5) A. Shonfield and S. Shaw (Ed.), Social Indicators
   Proceedings of joint Uk/USA SSRC conference held at Ditchley Park, Oxford May (1971), (contains a long bibliography), Heinemann, London (1971)

6) A. Campbell and P. Converse, Monitoring the Quality of American Life, Research proposal to the Russell Sage Foundation, New York (1970)

7) N. Bradburn, The Structure of Psychological Well-Being Aldinee Press, USA (1969)

8) J.P. Robinson and P.R. Shaver, Measures of Social Psychological Attitudes – I.S.R., Ann Arbor, Michigan (1970)

9) F.P. Kilpatrick and H. Cantril, Self-Anchoring Scaling: A Measure of Individuals Unique Reality Worlds, Journ. of Indiv. Psychology, Vol. 16 No.8, Nov. (1960)

10) M.Abrams and J. Hall, The Condition of the British People: Report on a Pilot Survey using Self-rating Scales, Paper to conference on „Social Indicators" jointly sponsored by the Social Science Research Councils of U. K. and U.S.A., May (1971)

The Development and Dissemination of
New Technologies – Their Positive and
Negative Aspects Regarding Quality of Life

TECHNOLOGY IN GLOBAL PERSPECTIVE

Some Results of the Club of Rome Project „On the Predicament of Mankind"

Peter Milling
Industrieseminar der Universität Mannheim
Mannheim, Federal Republic of Germany

I. Global Consequences of Technology

For many centuries technology provided the possibilities for mankind to overcome natural barriers and to allow a tremendous increase in population growth and industrial output. In the last decades negative side-effects of technical progress became obvious, and an awareness of possible dangers of uncontrolled technology arose. The desire for a formal technology assessment is one result of this awareness.

Critical developments which are not typical for some specific countries but which can be observed all over the globe caused the *Club of Rome,* an informal organization of approximately seventy leading personalities, to initiate a research programme to analyze the impact and the underlying causes of these developments. Funded by the Volkswagen Foundation, a group of scientists developed at the Massachusetts Institute of Technology (M.I.T.) a computer simulation model to study global problems. This work was based on a prototype model designed by Jay W. Forrester[1]. The results were published in a report for the Club of Rome under the title *„The Limits to Growth".* The main conclusion of this report are[2]:

1. „If the present growth trends in world population, industrialization, pollution, food production, and resource depletion continue unchanged, the limits to growth on this planet will be reached sometime within the next one hundred years. The most probable result will be a rather sudden and uncontrollable decline in both population and industrial capacity."

2. „It is possible to alter these growth trends and to establish a condition of ecological and economic stability that is sustainable far into the future. The state of global equilibrium could be designed so that the basic material needs of each person on earth are satisfied and each person has an equal opportunity to realize his individual human potential."

3. „If the world's people decide to strive for this second outcome rather than the first, the sooner they begin working to attain it, the greater will be their chances of succes"[2].

In the following I will briefly point out some impacts of technology, examine how technology may influence the behaviour of the mentioned simulation model, and what recommendations can be derived from that study for a rational technology assessment.

1. Population Growth

Over long periods of history, human populations grew only very slowly. A high death rate due to malnutrition, lack of medical care, etc. was compensated by a high birth rate. Less than half a century ago, this was also the situation in the so called developing countries. Then the application of modern medicine allowed a dramatic reduction of death rates. The birth rates, however, remained at their high level and thus the population growth rate jumped from values around zero percent to two, three or even more percent per year and led to rapidly growing populations. Technology also provided means to lower the birthrate to the desired one but traditional social attitudes change very slowly and the desired family size is still significantly above the number necessary for reproduction. This population growth undermined the attempts to increase the material wealth of the developing countries (see Figure 1).

2. Food Production

Arable land is only in limited supply on this globe, and a growing population requires a growing food production in order to provide the same amount of food per person. Out of about 3.2 billion (3.2×10^9)

Country	Population (1968) (million)	Average annual growth rate of population (1961–68) (% per year)	GNP per capita (1968) (US dollars)	Average annual growth rate of GNP per capita (1961–68) (% per year)
People's Republic of China	730	1.5	90	0.3
India	524	2.5	100	1.0
USSR	238	1.3	1,100	5.8
United States	201	1.4	3,980	3.4
Pakistan	123	2.6	100	3.1
Indonesia	113	2.4	100	0.8
Japan	101	1.0	1,190	9.9
Brazil	88	3.0	250	1.6
Nigeria	63	2.4	70	— 0.3
Federal Republic of Germany	60	1.0	1,970	3.4

Figure 1: Population Growth Rates and Economic Growth[3]

hectares of land suitable for agriculture on earth, approximately 50% is under cultivation.

The remaining half is of very much lower quality and would require immense capital investment to clear, irrigate, fertilize, etc. before it could be used. Even when we assume that this money would be made available, food production is limited. On an average, 0.4 hectares per person are needed to grow the food he is consuming (for the current U.S. standards, 0.9 hectares per person are required). In Figure 2, the lower curve shows the amount of land needed to feed the world population which is growing by 2.1 per cent per year; the upper curve shows the actual amount of arable land available which decreases over time since each additional person requires a certain amount of land for housing, roads, power lines, waste disposal, etc. (0.008 hectares are assumed here). The dotted lines show arable land needed if technological progress allows a doubling or a

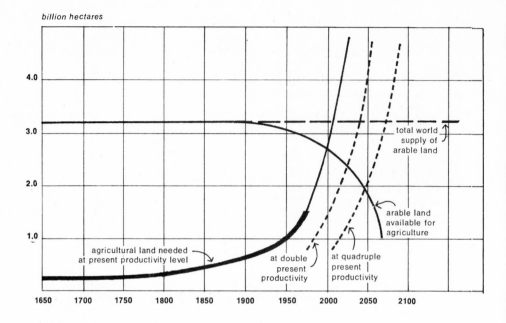

Figure 2: Arable Land

quadrupling of productivity. The intercept between these lines and the curve of arable land available are delayed by only 30 years.

Within very few years one moves from a situation of great abundance of land to one of great scarcity. As long as technology does not provide a faster growth in productivity ad infinitum, it only delays that development.

Even the tremendous increase in agricultural productivity during the last decade — the so called Green Revolution — did not provide more food per capita in the developing countries than in 1956. The rapidly growing population absorbed all additional food supply (Figure 3). In fact, the situation worsened even, since now a larger number of people is starving than before.

3. Environmental Pollution

The drastic increase in fertilizer consumption, resource depletion, industrial output, etc. was not without severe impact on the environment. The
serious damages man has done to the ecological system are well known. I
refer only to the energy problem which is often overlooked when
potential technological solutions are discussed.

Figure 4 shows the relationship between energy consumption and GNP
per capita. The same relationship is certainly valid when, instead of GNP
per capita, the level of technological sophistication is plotted on the
abscissa. Even if we assume that there will be no energy shortage − by
means of controlled fusion, for instance − we are still faced with the

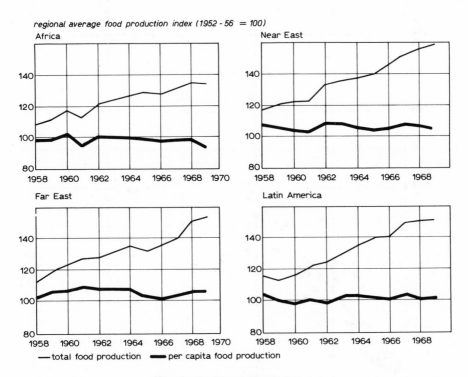

Figure 3: Food Production

fundamental law of thermodynamics that all generated energy finally ends up as heat.

A more sophisticated technology can be expected to require more energy and the problem of 'thermal pollution' will worsen; it effects local climates already now. When technology is applied to solve a pollution problem, the problem is likely to be only shifted from one pollutant to another, namely to thermal pollution.

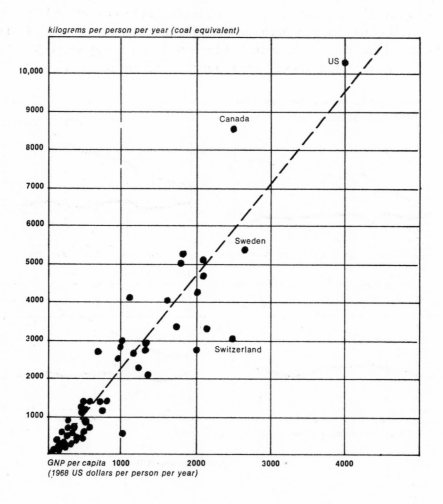

Figure 4: Energy Consumption and GNP per capita

II. Technology and Physical Limits to Growth

To examine the complex dynamic interactions of the quoted developments and several others, the M.I.T. group designed a computer simulation
model using the System Dynamics approach[4]. The diagram-representa-
tion of this model is shown in Figure 5. If we assume no major changes
in the physical, economic, or social relationships that have historically
governed the development of the world system, the model generates the
behaviour shown in Figure 6. Food, industrial output per capita, and
population grow exponentially until the rapidly diminishing natural resources force a slowdown in industrial growth.

After a delay, population growth is halted and then turns negative due to
decreased food and medical services.

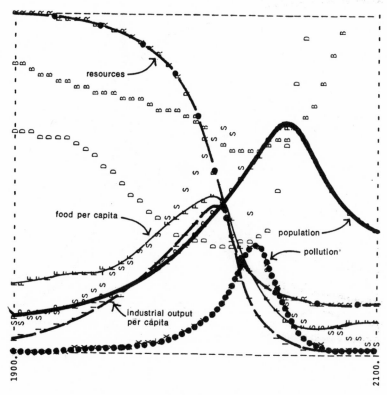

Figure 6: World Model, Standard Run

116

The technologist's response to such a development would, for example, be to seek for technologies which allow a more efficient use of available resources and to utilize lower grade ores and to mine the seabed. If these changes are introduced in the model, growth is stopped by rising pollution (Figure 7).

We now add a further technological improvement to the model to avoid resource depletion and pollution problems which determined the collapse modes in the previous model runs. We assume that pollution generation per unit of agricultural and industrial output can be reduced in 1975 to one fourth of its 1970 value (Figure 8).

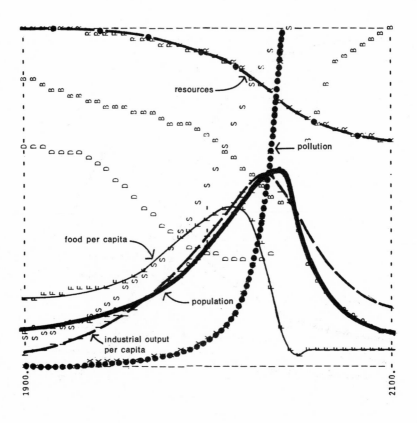

Figure 7: World model with 'unlimited' resources

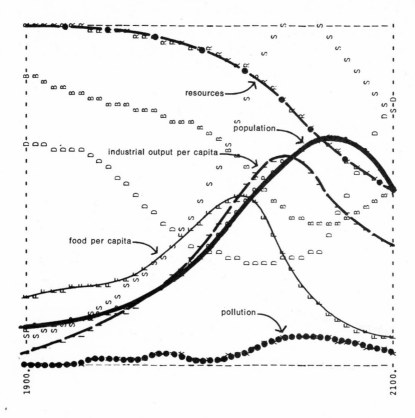

Figure 8: World model with 'unlimited' resources and pollution controls

These changes allow population and industry to grow until the limit of arable land is reached. Food per capita declines, and industrial growth is also slowed down as capital is diverted to food production.

The problem as it stands now is either too little food or too many people. The technological response to the first situation would be to produce more food, to the second to provide better methods of birth control.

In Figure 9, four simultaneous technological policies are introduced into the model in an attempt to avoid the behaviour of previous runs: Even low grade resources are fully exploited, and 75 % of those used are recycled; pollution generation is reduced to one-fourth; land yields are doubled, and

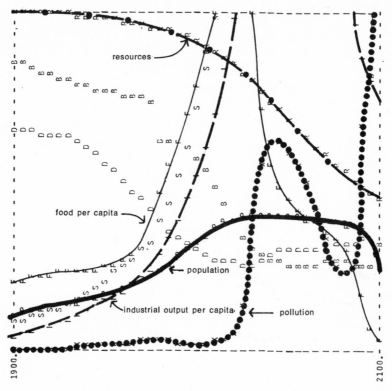

Figure 9: World model with 'unlimited' resources, pollution controls, increased agricultural productivity, and 'perfect' birth control

effective methods of birth control are made available to the world population.

The result of these policies is a temporary achievement of a constant population with a high world average income per capita. Finally, however, industrial growth is halted, and the death rate rises as resources are depleted, pollution accumulates, and food production declines.

Technology relieves the symptons of a problem without affecting the underlying causes. It thus delays only the critical developments or shifts to new problems. The basic cause of all the quoted problems is simple — exponential growth of physical goods cannot go on for ever in a finite environment. Therefore, technology can possibly be applied with more satisfying results than shown in the computer plots (and the model is capable to generate these behaviour modes) but we cannot expect technology to solve all our problems. It has to be made very clear, however, that technology is absolutely essential for society and we have to accept certain negative side-effects in the industrialized countries. But we have to recognize that there are limits and that especially a rapidly growing population will lead to a faster reaching of these limits.

III. Requirements of Technology Assessments

It occurs to me that there are three basic facts which are relevant for technology assessment and each of them should be examined carefully in the process of assessing a new technology.

1. Technological Potentials and Social Receptivity

Technology, when applied to social systems, frequently offers only the *potential* to improve a specific situation. The pure availability of new technology has in most cases no effect until it is applied properly and accepted by society. The prime example here are modern contraceptives which offer a chance for perfect birth control. The social receptiveness in those parts of the world where they are most urgently needed, namely in the developing countries, is, however, missing. Many family planning projects failed because of the lacking intellectual capabilities to apply the contraceptives properly and, more important, because of the desire for many children. Technology advances very rapidly, traditional meta-economic value systems change very slowly. Before the application of modern medicine, it was necessary to give birth to a large number of children since only a view would survive and take care of their parents in their old days. Before the changed situation is perceived the birth rate will remain at its high level.

2. Short Term versus Long Term Objective Function

Rational technological assessment should employ an objective function with a time horizon which goes beyond the short term problems we are facing. When costs and benefit are distributed unevenly over time, frequently the discounted net present value is used as a basis for decision making. This procedure, however, assigns essentially zero value to anything more than twenty years from now. Due to the long delays in social and ecological systems, negative side-effects of technologies become obvious only after a long incubation time. DDT, for example, is used since the early fourties, and it took nearly thirty years before ecological damages through the application of this chemical became widely known. But even when we know that DDT is harmful for the environment, the decision to be made must consider side-effects and long term consequences and must weight them against the short term benefits. When DDT is banned now, this may cause danger to approximately 1,3 billion people which could be threatened by malaria[5]. The fact that they can live safely today may very well outweigh the cost imposed on future generations through the continued use of chemicals. But at least the trade-offs should be pointed out and analyzed.

3. The Complexity of Social Systems

Social systems are of complex nature where a multitude of interdependencies exist between variables. These complex interdependencies have to be considered, and technology assessment should employ a system's view on nature. 'Complex system' as used here refers to high order, multi-loop, non-linear feedback structure. All social systems belong to this class[6]. These systems have many important behaviour characteristics which must be understood if we expect to influence their behavior through technology. Among these characteristics are

(1) A remarkable insensitivity to changes in many system parameters.
(2) A stubborn resistance against policy changes.
(3) A counteraction and compensation for externally applied corrective efforts by reducing corresponding internally generated action.
(4) A reaction to a policy change in a long run which is opposite to how they react in the short run.

As an example, how the use of technology caused short term benefits and long term disadvantages, we may look at modern whaling. Whalers have systematically reached one limit after the other and have attempted to overcome each one by applying more sophisticated technology (Figure

121

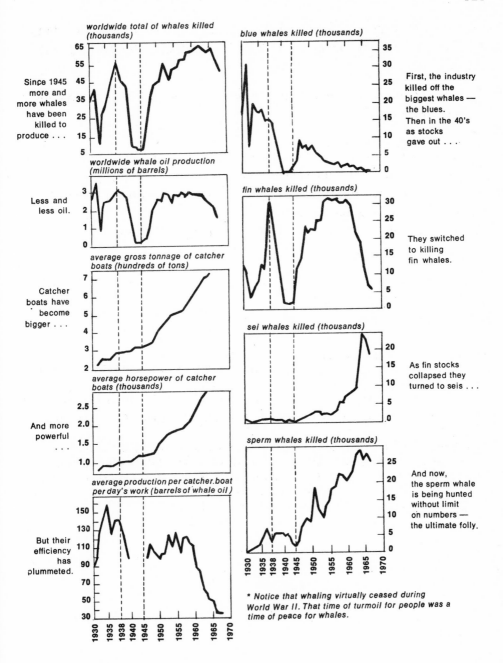

Figure 10: Modern Whaling

10). As a result, they have whiped out one whale species after another but the final outcome of this policy is a final extinction of both whales and whalers.

As a brief summary I would like to refer to the basic assumptions of ecology which read

1. Everything is connected to everything else.
2. Everything must go somewhere.
3. There is no such thing as a free lunch — not even with the help of the most sophisticated technology.

Technology assessment must consider these interrelationships.

References and Remarks:

1) J.W. Forrester, World Dynamics, Cambridge, Mass. (1971)
2) D.H. Meadows, et al., The Limits to Growth, New York, N.Y. (1972)
3) Figure 1 and the following Figures are taken from Ref. 2.
4) For a comprehensive description of this approach see J.W. Forrester, Industrial Dynamics, Cambridge, Mass. (1961) and Principles of Systems, Cambridge, Mass. (1969)
5) J. Randers and D.H. Meadows, The Carrying Capacity of our Global Environment: A Look at the Ethical Alternatives, in: D.L. Meadows and D.H. Meadows (eds.), Toward Global Equilibrium: Collected Papers, Cambridge, Mass. (1973), p. 330
6) See J.W. Forrester, Urban Dynamics, Cambridge, Mass. (1969) p. 107
7) B. Commoner, The Closing Circle, Doubleday (1971)

THE PROCESS OF INTERNATIONAL DISSEMINATION OF NEW TECHNOLOGY WITH REGARD TO QUALITY OF LIFE

Nadezda Grubor

Institute of International Politics and Economics
Belgrade, Yugoslavia

The contemporary progress of science and technology has opened new undreamed perspectives of the development of human society with the new possibilities to solve its most important and crucial economic and social problems. It depends on many factors, amongst which an easy access to the new technology for the underdeveloped countries is the most important because they depend to a large extent on the foreign techno- logy. This fact determines the significance of the *transfer of new technology* in the general process of international dissemination of new technology and its connections with the question of *quality of life.*

The underdeveloped countries are unable to develop their own scientific and technological base without external assistance. This failure leads to the phenomenon of the technological gap that is gradually widening. The actual independence of the underdeveloped countries is not possible under conditions of technological dependence.

While developed countries have the problem of quality of life, as they solved the problem of insufficient quantity of material consumer goods, the underdeveloped countries are facing both quantity and quality problems, bearing in mind the experience of the developed countries.

How to prevent the appearance of the negative side effects of the applications of new technology and keep the positive ones?

It seems that there is only one possible way: to coordinate efforts of mankind as a whole. Naturally the primary role is that of the underdeveloped countries themselves, but the aid of developed countries is irreplaceable.

The need of a coordinated national and international action in the field of technology transfer to the underdeveloped countries is evident and recognized by many competent institutions. This question was discussed in the course of the Third session of the UNCTAD (April-May 1972, Santiago, Chile):

„As regards the international transfer of technology, the Conference has decided, inter alia, that the continuing nature of UNCTAD's functions in this field should be reflected in the institutional arangements in UNCTAD. It adopted a series of recommendations concerning measures to improve the transfer of and access to technology, addressed to developing countries, developed market economy countries and the socialist countries of Eastern Europe, as well as to the international community at large in respect of the special position of the least developed among developing countries; it endorsed the work programme of the Intergovernmental group on the transfer of technology[1].

The future will show whether it will be accomplished. It seems there are two main aims within the framework of the problem of international transfer of technology:

1. The formation of authentic technology developing capability in the underdeveloped countries

2. The diffusion of a technology throughout the economy by policies encouraging more rapid diffusion.

Technology advance forces the underdeveloped countries to find the most appropriate way to keep up with other countries under all circumstances with or without paying attention to the question of quality of life.

While it is impossible, this time to explain the very different opinions about the concept of international transfer of new technology because this field is relatively new and unclear, it is more useful to underline the common basic points that will prove necessity of an urgent assistance by more advanced countries.

(1) New technology is necessary to accelerate economic and social development of the underdeveloped countries without any doubt.

(2) International transfer of new technology is an extremely complex process and requires specific decisions for each individual case. There is not a general model, all cases have specific features.

(3) The process of international dissemination of new technology always depends on the personal capabality of the man involved, and because of that, special attention has to be paid to permanent adequate training of the labor force.

(4) International transfer of new technology has to be followed by development of an internal R&D sector, that is able to accept the foreign technology and to develop a national innovative capacity. This is necessary first of all because the foreign technology, i.e. the object of the transfer, is new in a relative sense only. In the contrary case, the recipient country will be condemned to a permanent lag.

(5) The necessary precondition for successful transfer of new technology is the aid to the underdeveloped countries in every phase of this process (choice, financing, adaptation, development, function) in order to remove possible obstacles.

(6) The transfer of new technology must be done with extreme caution and taking full account of the possible changes in socio-psychological structures to prevent the appearence of the new problems of psychological and sociological nature that are more complex than pure technical problems. In this context the question of quality of life is to be investigated.

Finally I will quote a part of the statement by Mr. Raul Prebisch, Under-Secretary-General of the United Nations at the Third session of UNCTAD:

„We are at a great turning-point in history, whose implications are profound and where the course of events could either throw up new concepts of zones of influence from north to south, or else help to fulfil the noble aim of bringing the developing countries economic and political independence[2].

This is not possible without effective assistance of whole mankind, because the danger of misusing new technology is a general one. The process of the transfer of technology is based on two persons: one is donor and the other is recipient, but the responsibility for a succesful process is of the whole international community.

References:

1) Report of the UNCTAD on its Third session, UNCTAD TD/178, July 27, (1972)

2) Statement by Mr. Raul Prebisch, TD/156, April 29, (1972)

The Process of Industrial and Agricultural Production and its Impact on Quality of Life

THE INDUSTRIAL PROCESS AND THE QUALITY OF LIFE

James S. Wilson
Glasgow College of Technology
Glasgow, United Kingdom

Introduction

Perhaps the most appropriate starting point for this paper is a disclaimer. Although the discussion is fundamentally concerned with the problems normally associated with what economists like to call 'structural unemployment', the definition of unemployment used here is rather broader than that normally accepted by labour economists. Moreover, and perhaps partly at least as a consequence, the difficult analytical problems involved in isolating 'structural unemployment' and its direct implications are mentioned rather more briefly than they deserve. In mitigation, I would plead that an interdisciplinary seminar such as this, is not necessarily the best place to indulge in what are primarily disputes of interest mainly to the professional economist.

Although economics is the social science perhaps nearest the core of any problem concerning the 'quality of life', the value of a group discussion such as this lies in the possibilities which it offers for the exchange of views on broad areas which are of common concern to us all rather than indulgence in isolated specialist quibbles. It is — to borrow a simile — akin to an intellectual pub crawl with the only free house being that of the economist precisely because of the focal role held by economics.

The basic premise of this paper is therefore that the quality of life of any individual or community can in a direct and simple way be related to income — the music of Mozart (even in Salzburg) is arguably less attractive to a starving man. Since unemployment statistics reflect mainly the inability of people to 'earn their living', this view of the quality of life is rather negative but nevertheless vital.

The paper is in three parts. *Part I* discusses very briefly the problems involved in identifying the role played by the industrial process in creating unemployment, and some tentative hypotheses are set up. *Part II* describes the area studied and presents the evidence which is currently available. *Part III* then attempts to summarize the problem without insisting on dogmatic conclusions.

Part I: Some analytical Problems

In order to demonstrate that the 'industrial process' has affected the quality of life thus defined, it is obviously necessary to distinguish between unemployment created by deficiencies in the level of aggregate demand and unemployment which is caused directly by changes in the structure of the demand for labour. Unemployment which falls into the first category can by definition be alleviated by expansionary monetary and fiscal policies operated by the central government. Structural unemployment however is ipso facto not so responsive to such policies[1] and is usually thought to require additional labour market policies such as increased expenditure on employment services, training grants etc. Given that such labour market policies involve expenditure of considerable sums of money[2] these policies, it may be argued, will be continued up to the point where the social benefits (i.e. reducing the level of unemployment) just equals the costs of the policies[3].

There has been considerable controversy over whether unemployment is wholly demand deficient or whether structural unemployment caused by changes in technology altering the structure of demand for labour is important[4].

The intricacies of the debate need not concern us here, but in order to justify the premise on which this article is based, namely that it is the operation of the industrial process which is the main cause of unemployment in the area of Scotland under consideration, several points must be made.

First of all, at aggregate level, despite the difficulties in forming tests which are capable of distinguishing satisfactorily between the two kinds of unemployment, two arguments are clear. Firstly, if increasing structural employment does form a significant part of total unemployment, then when aggregate demand is inflated to equal aggregate supply, unemployment will be higher than at previous periods when this was the case. Secondly, in a more extreme version of the structuralist argument, given rigid wages (or at least wages which are less flexible downwards than upwards) periods when aggregate demand equals aggregate supply should be periods of substantial wage inflation. In the first case we hypothesize that this *is* the case and some preliminary work down on the Scottish economy certainly seems to confirm this as is shown below; in the second case it can be argued, though so far as is known to the author it has not yet been tested, that this *is* indeed true of the British economy as a whole.

The second main point follows from this, and it has important implications for regional analysis of unemployment. It has been shown[5] that the aggregate wage adjustment function has moved to the right since 1923 and several attempts have been made to explain this in terms of lax monetary and fiscal policies[6], trade union militancy[7], distribution of productivity increases[8].

In a study using disaggregated data, however, Thirlwall[9] has made the interesting observation that the ranking of regional wage functions by the intercept on the X-axis seems to agree almost exactly with their ranking in terms of the significance of the degree of structural unemployment in each, proposed by Brechling[10]. In other words, there is some evidence of structural unemployment in some regions being considerably more significant than it is at aggregate level[6].

As has been indicated above, some preliminary work done in the College in terms of the Scottish economy seems to confirm that structural employment seems to be an important and *growing problem*. If this is the case then it is extremely disturbing since over this period Scotland has been a 'development area' receiving special government assistance.

The importance of this section is that it establishes the basis for two hypotheses which are considered in this study and will be tested with more detailed data as the project progresses.

1. At greater levels of disaggregation of data (Clydebank) structural unemployment is a much more serious problem than it *seems* to be at the national level.

2. The Government policy towards 'development areas' may not be helping this problem at all in practice.

A final hypothesis which is being considered at this point though it is not yet tested, is that where structural unemployment is significant at the local level institutional factors may cause demand deficient unemployment to become structural in character, as unprofitable firms over-due for closure may close in the down-swing of the trade cycle and total unemployment would not necessarily respond to expansionary fiscal and monetary policies. If this is an acceptable hypothesis then *any* alteration of the situation by expanding aggregate demand would only be a short run palliative hiding longer run structural unemployment. It should be noted that this view run counter to the more traditional appraisal which emphasizes hidden demand deficient unemployment due to labour hoarding[11]. It should be noted that this view considers unemployment from the view point of causes rather than remedies and hence is rather broader than the usually accepted definition of structural unemployment. For convenience we will therefore call this 'process unemployment'[12].

Part II: A Local Case Study

Clydebank, which till recently was probably best known for the ships produced in its old established ship-yards, is now famous for a rather different reason — the 'work-in' at the John Brown's shipyard of the U.C.S. group over the 'right to work'.

In July 1961 the total work force in the burgh was just over 40,000 and the unemployment rate was 1.7%. By July 1970 the work force had fallen to just over 33,000 and unemployment stood at 5.8% of the total work force.

In short, over the period covered by this study, the total work force fell by 17% while unemployment rose from rather less than the national

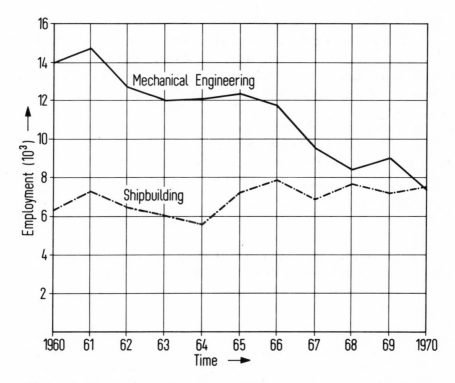

Figure 1: Employment Patterns in Mechanical Engineering and Ship-building in Clydebank 1960-1970

average to well above it. The limited local data currently available seems to show the same characteristics as those for the Scottish economy from 1950 — 1970, and conform to the pattern which we would expect if structural unemployment (narrowly defined) was a significant factor.

It is the basic premise of this paper that reliance on the mechanical engineering and ship-building and repairing industries, as shown in Table 1, has led to this situation being exacerbated by what we have called 'process unemployment', and the purpose of the paper is to study the effects of this on the area in terms of four variables:

(1) Migration from the area.
(2) Employment in retail shops.
(3) Rent arrears in tenants of council houses.
(4) Number of students enrolled for engineering courses at the local technical college.

Table 1: Estimated employment pattern as % total working population in Clydebank by major industries 1960 — 1970:

Industry	Estimated Employment		
	1960 %	1965 %	1970 %
Food, Drink and Tobacco	3.0	4.0	6.3
Mechanical Engineering	51.0	42.2	30.5
Ship-building & Marine Engineering	17.3	20.2	21.2
Construction	3.0	4.0	4.6
Professional & Scientific Services	3.0	4.1	7.1
Distributive Trades	6.0	9.1	9.3

As has been noted above, the unemployment figures for the burgh show 'structural' tendencies similar to those for Scotland as a whole. The difference between the successive dips in unemployment in 1966 and

1970 is rather greater than for the Scottish economy though the linear trend in unemployment is remarkably similar.

Although detailed data showing the analysis of unemployment by length of time out of work is only available for the three years since 1969, one study[13] has estimated that the average period out of work in Clydebank has lengthened from 6 weeks in 1965 to 6 months in 1972, and the data which is available shows that the percentage of the work force unemployed for more than eight weeks has risen from 59.9.% in July 1969 to 67.9% in July 1972.

It also seems probable that the size of this problem is understated in the official figures because of married women who are made redundant failing to register as unemployed. Thus from an all time low in July 1966, female unemployment had risen by 83 in July 1970, while female employment figures had fallen by 301[14].

Much of the increase in unemployment was caused by falling demand for labour by the two main industries, mechanical engineering and shipbuilding and repairing, which in 1970 accounted for over 50% of the total jobs available. The fall in employment by these two is illustrated in Figure 1. Moreover, it seems that the main burden fell on the unskilled workers, especially so in shipbuilding as would perhaps be expected. Thus in June 1972, unskilled workers represented 47.8% of the total unemployed in Clydebank, but 60.7% of the unemployed who had last worked in shipbuilding[15]. Over the period under consideration the unemployed unskilled shipyard workers formed between 55% and 70% of the total unemployed in this industry. If this is true of the other main industry — and there seems some casual evidence that this is the case — a working hypothesis would seem to be that the burden of the unemployment is falling more and more severely on those who by definition are least able to benefit from central government labour market policies such as retraining. It may also be hypothesized (though this is commented on at a later stage) that where technical change is directly responsible for unemployment, i.e. narrowly defined structural employment, that this grade of worker will become less required by industry.

Some specific effects of unemployment can now be considered briefly.

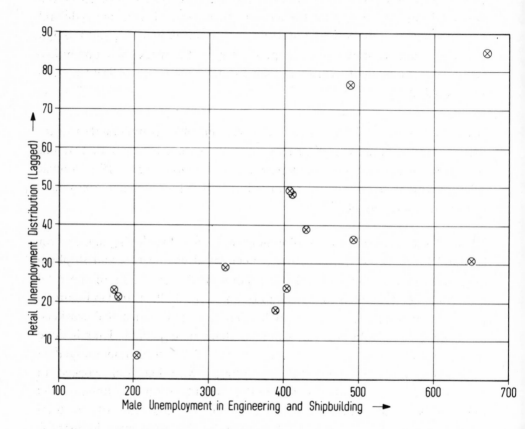

Figure 2: Relationship between Unemployed in Engineering and Shipbuilding and Retailing Unemployment (1 year lag) 1960-1972

Migration

The reasoning here is straightforward and tells a tale not unknown in Scotland. It simply states that where specific groups of people are persistently affected by high unemployment rates (or even more generally, where there is a lack of job opportunities though this has not yet been tested) that people tend to leave their homes in search of work.

Two points should be borne in mind here. First of all the problem of obtaining data for migration necessitated the use of total insured population as proxy variable. This is not entirely satisfactory but is a useful guide. Secondly, in this study data for *all* variables considered was limited, and hence any conclusions must be tentative, and await further tests when more data becomes available.

The relatioship $y_t = d + BU_t + B_2 Y_t - 1$ was found to be a reasonably good fit given the limited data, and a correlation coefficient of 0.6 (n=11), was obtained, were

Y_t = current number of insured population

U_t = current male unemployment. Male unemployment data was used because of the female non-registering.

$Y_t - 1$ = insured population in period $t - 1$.

In other words it would seem to be a useful hypothesis that peoples' expectations about the unemployment situation is one factor influencing the level of migration out of the area[16]. In terms of the quality of life in that community therefore, this means that high unemployment, i.e. the inability to obtain work is a highly significant factor. However, this denuding of working population from the main employing industries will arguably have a multiplier effect on other industries. An example of this is tested in the next variable.

Employment in retail shops

As has been argued, this variable attempts to indicate the significance of the effect on employment in shops of unemployment in the major industries. The process by which this is seen as affecting the quality of life

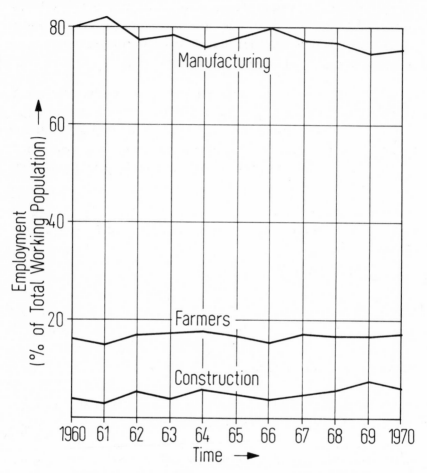

Figure 3: Employment in Clydebank (1960-1970)

is simply that reduced spending by unemployed workers will be reflected in employment in retail shops.

For practical purposes the effects of selective employment tax imposed in 1966 on service employment is ignored. The only reason for this is that in the Glasgow area as a whole service employment appears to have risen over the six years since 1966, while in Clydebank it rose till 1967 then trailed off. When the hypothesis is tested later in the project allowance will be made for this effect. (The position is illustrated in Figures 2 and 3).

Preliminary examination of the data seems to show that there is in fact an effect one year later of unemployment in the single industries on unemployment in the retail sector. While this is perhaps only to be expected it is interesting to note that there seems to be a switch in spending away from retail purchases and hence arguably the quality of life in the community falls.

Rent Arrears

The reasoning here is that expenditure on house rents is a necessity of life, and failure to pay rents reflects a pressure through falling income on the quality of life. Again subject to data limitations, there appears to be a meaningful relationship between unemployment and rent arrears in the same period. In other words, we are hypothesizing that unemployment strikes immediately at the basic necessities of a minimum standard of living for the workers in the area. It can of course be argued that the choice not to pay rents reflects the social security system of granting rent allowances. While this may be a significant factor not allowed for here, it still seems to be true that the arrears are purely temporary, and do in fact tend to disappear as unemployment slows down[17].

Intake of Trainee Students at the Local College

This is the final variable to be considered. Unfortunately, the College is very new as it only opened in 1965, and hence any meaningful regression analysis is impossible. The scatter diagram showing the postulated relationships between intake of full-time students from the engineering and

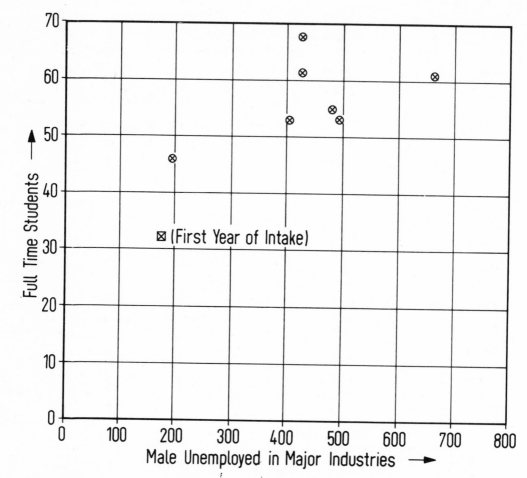

Figure 4: Relationship between Unemployment and Full Time Student Intake

shipbuilding industry and unemployment in the industries is shown in Figure 3. The hypothesis is that full time student numbers will tend to increase as job availability becomes limited. It is also arguable that higher unemployment means fewer opportunities for students being sponsored by their firms and this seems to be the case in the years of rapid increase in unemployment in 1969-72. Even given the inadequacies of the data it seems arguable that the relationship shows some vindication of this hypothesis and should be followed up in the future. The implication of the diagram is of course that those who *are* in employment in periods of high unemployment suffer and that firms are unwilling to engage young people to train them thereby limiting their chances of emerging from the lower skilled grades in the immediate future with the possible consequences of possible early redundancy already discussed.

Part III: Some tentative Conclusions and their Implications

While much more work requires to be done some interesting hypotheses can be formed at this stage.

(1) Structural or process unemployment as defined in this paper seems to be a more serious problem in this area than at aggregate level.

(2) The problem is probably understated in the official figures by married women failing to register as unemployed. This is perhaps more significant for this area than for many as the female participation rate for the Glasgow area is higher than any other urban conurbation in the United Kingdom.

(3) The groups which seem to suffer most are those least likely to benefit easily from traditional government labour market policies and indeed their position is arguably becoming more serious as the average length of time unemployed seems to indicate.

(4) Given that Clydebank has throughout the whole period been part of a development area, this failure to alleviate unemployment may reflect on regional policy as much as labour market policy. Ths is briefly discussed below.

(5) The variables considered seem to indicate that:
(a) the expectation of unemployment has a direct effect in determining the level of migration and hence the total size of the community and through a multiplier effect the pattern of employment.
(b) Insofar as the quality of life can be inferred from changes in the level of income there is some evidence that unemployment exerts a direct influence through expenditure on necessities.
(c) Unemployment also seems to reflect changes in employer willingness to allow time for employees to gain the qualifications which it can be argued are necessary to the problems of gaining employment away from the unskilled.

If these arguments are accepted they have two main implications which must now be briefly considered. The first of these concerns the problem of predicting changes in the demand for labour. This is obviously a necessary prerequisite for any policy which seeks to devise methods of controlling and alleviating its effects. Unfortunately, this poses considerable methodological problems for the economist as the pressure is basically one of *change*. Thus it is arguable that current attempts to use changes in the capital factor in the economists' Cobb-Douglas production function to illustrate the effects of changes in capital intensity[18] (i.e. here technical change) to predict changes in the demand for labour at the level of the firm, are using a *static* methodology to tackle a *dynamic* problem. It is certainly true, however, that it is at this micro level of analysis which the most useful contribution to detailed study of the manpower effects of technical change could be made. To state a problem is now to solve it but some work here by theoretical economists would probably pay rich dividends in terms of greater understanding of the problems of structural unemployment.

The final point considered here is the role of government regional policy. Since 1966 part of the government regional policy has involved payments of *grants* to firms in development areas, except for a short period over 1970 — 1971. In 1972 the Government, however, ended payment of regional employment premiums to firms.

Both of these measures were designed to alleviate unemployment in the regions by assisting firms financially and also attracting new firms into the regions. If the hypothesis put forward in this paper that their seems to be hidden structural unemployment proves tenable, then it is arguable that the attraction of industry to the regions should become more selective for two reasons. First of all payment of grants to unprofitable firms would on a priori grounds appear to exacerbate the 'process unemployment' problem as has been argued. Secondly the problem of forecasting the demand from new firms with different technologies for labour in the local market as acute and one which we have argued requires much more study.

Conclusions

Perhaps the only conclusion a paper such as this can come to is that in the area under consideration structural problems caused by changes in the industrial processes employed do seem to cause problems which are not entirely amendable solely to manipulation of aggregate demand by the central government. Moreover, as these problems affect the level of income of the individual e.g. in the variables specified and hence the quality of his life and that of the community we have defined a problem which is worthy of much more detailed investigation.

References and Remarks

1) Though see e.g. Technology, Economic Growth and Public Policies, Nelson et al, Brookings Institution (1967) p. 140-141

2) The efficiency of such policies is a side issue here but of some importance in deciding how best to minimize the effects of structural unemployment, and as yet has been the subject of little research in the U.K. See e.g. Government Manpower Policies in Great Britain A.P. Thirlwall, July (1972)

3) See e.g. R.G. Lipsey, Structural and Demand Deficient Unemployment Reconsidered in Employment Policy and the Labour Market, ed. Ross, (1965)

4) See e.g. Lipsey; especially in U.K. the most recent forecasts by Ball and Burns of London Business School (S.T. 27/8/72) seem to imply (though for rather curious reasons) that they consider the basic problem to be deficient demand.

5) See Lipsey, Relationships between Unemployment and Rate of Change of Money Wages in U.K. 1962-1957.

6) See Bronfenn Brenner, A Sample Survey of the Commission on Money and Credit Research Papers, Review of Economics and Statistics, February Supplement (1963)

7) See Hines, Unemployment and Rate of Change of Money Wages in U.K., A Repraisal, Review of Economics and Statistics (1963)

8) See R.J. Bele, Inflation and the Theory of Money, Allen & Unwin (1964)

9) Thirlwall shows that zero inflation, at *aggregate level* would require 4.4 per cent unemployment, while in terms of the Scottish Economy approximately 7 per cent unemployment would be required. If, however, there were no dispersion in the adjustment function then only 1.8 per cent unemployment would be required at the aggregate level. See Oxford University, Bulletin of Economics and Statistics (1968)

10) See F. Breckling, Oxford Economic Papers (1969)

11) Testing of this hypothesis will be part of the larger project.

12) Current research at Sussex University which seem to show that the pace of technical change in the engineering industry is slow (and likely to continue to be so) and hence unlikely to raise any spectres of massive structural unemployment is not necessarily at odds with the argument in this paper. The fact that employment *has* fallen significantly the engineering industry in Clydebank is indisputable and the research point that retraining is continually necessary supports our hypothesis that *after people have been* redundant the labour market mechanism is unlikely even in periods of expansion to allocate them to a job for which they have been trained and hence the problem of rising unskilled unemployment remains. See fig. 1.

13) A. Buchan, The Right to Work, Caldar & Boyars (1972)

14) See also Bosanquet and Standing, B.J.I.R., July (1972)

15) Figures for Engineering are not yet available.

16) It is true of course that certain ethnic groups such as coal miners do not seem to conform to this behaviour pattern.

17) This is an assertion by the housing factor for the area. It was however maintained that this was the case under questioning.

18) See e.g. The effects of an advance in Technology on Employment in a Industry: A Structural Model: L. Burman, in Engineering Economist Vol. 14 no. 4 (1972)

THE IMPACT OF WORK AND ENVIRONMENT ON WORK MOTIVATION*)

Rudolph A. C. Bruyns
Frederik Muller Akademie
Amsterdam, Netherlands

The research findings which are often really or seemingly contradictory and the desire to arrive at an integration of the existing concepts about human behaviour in the work situation are the reasons which have led us to make *work motivation* and *job satisfaction* once more the subject of a study, in spite of the multiplicity of previous studies on this matter. Another reason for this study is that we cannot escape the impression that owing to a lack of insight the personnel policy adopted in work organizations (insofar as its coordination with work orientation existing in employees is concerned) is not flexible enough and pays too little regard to social and technological developments.

This study contains a report on two investigations. The first investigation dealt with personnel (all levels) employed with the chemical works of DSM. The second investigation related to members of the ,,Centrum voor Hoger Personeel (CHP) (Senior Staff Centre) of the 'N.V.V.' (Dutch Trade Union).

Although the two investigations, either by themselves or combined, were suited for verifying a number of hypotheses of the same tenor, each of them had a special objective. The purpose of the *DSM investigation* (the immediate investigation) was to verify in particular those hypotheses which relate to differences in work motivation and job satisfaction between categories of employees defined by hierarchical level (as regards

---

*) Summary of a Thesis published in Dutch by van Gorcum & Co. N. V., Assen, Netherlands

actual work situation, class and training), whilst use is made of the same method of investigation and a number of factors are kept under control. The purpose of the *CHP investigation* was rather to examine what role is played by such factors as training, origin, job, etc., within one and the same 'professional environment' (class) in the creation of a certain motivation structure and job satisfaction. The hypotheses to be verified. were based on the assumption that differences existing between employees in work orientation (= motivation structure), willingness to work (= willingness to achieve a minimum performance or a more than minimum performance) and job satisfaction, in addition to differences in personality structure, may be attributed to the differentiation in socio-cultural environment and actual work situation between employees.

Since personality characteristics as well as characteristics of the actual work situation and the pertinent socio-cultural environment manifest themselves through positions occupied by the individual, the influence of these intervening variables on work orientation, willingness to work and work satisfaction has been examined by analysis of the relation between positional characteristics and the differences existing between individuals in work motivation and job satisfaction. In the investigations we have confined ourselves to some positional characteristics, such as occupational class, level of training, age, marital status, tenure, native district, social environment of origin and trade union membership. The fact that we have confined ourselves to these positions and refrained from including positions, for example, within political organizations, family, local community, leisure-time activities, etc., is due to the circumstance that on the one hand the positions which have been included in the discussions can easily be obtained and ascertained objectively from a research technical point of view, and that on the other it is not actually these positions that are of importance in this respect, but the influence of the three intervening variables. On the basis of the problems as formulated and the hypotheses derived from them, we have drawn up a list of questions which measure:

(1) the structure of work motivation (what aspects in the work'situation are considered by the employee important as work motive?);

(2) the extent to which motivating aspects are to be found in the work situation concerned;

(3) the willingness to perform the amount of work dictated by hierarchy in the work situation involved (based on the job involvement scale of Lodahl and Kejner);

(4) the willingness to perform work not essential from the financial point of view, independently of the work situation involved;

(5) satisfaction with the job itself and satisfaction with the entire work situation.

In the DSM investigation, 229 of the 260 interviews were found to be suitable for processing. The four respective subgroups to be considered for analysis — operatives, junior staff, intermediate staff and senior staff — proved not to deviate from the originally stratified random sample insofar as personality characteristics are concerned which are kept under control (age, years of service, tenure (company and present function), mobility criterium, trade union membership.
In the CHP investigation, 210 individuals selected at random, all holding positions which in the trade union concerned are reckoned among the senior staff positions, had filled out the questionnaire completely.

The research findings lead to the following *conclusions:*
(1) The usual distinction between a job intrinsic and job extrinsic work orientation is too inflexible. Work situation aspects relating to human relations and wage/promotion opportunities prove to form a separate factor in work orientation and not to fall under the job extrinsic and job instrinsic categories. As a matter of fact, four aspect areas may be distinguished (here the (irrelevant) status aspects and the aspects of leadership are neglected), viz.,

— aspects relating to work environment and conditions of employment (purely extrinsic aspects);
— aspects relating to autonomy (purely intrinsic aspects);
— aspects relating to self-actualization/scope (in view of the highly positive correlation with the „autonomy" aspects revealed by the investigation and in accordance with Herzberg's distinction between 'intrinsic' and 'extrinsic' these aspects must also be interpreted as purely intrinsic);
— aspects relating to human relations and to wages and promotion.

Schematically, the correlation between the four above mentioned areas of aspects could be outlined as follows:

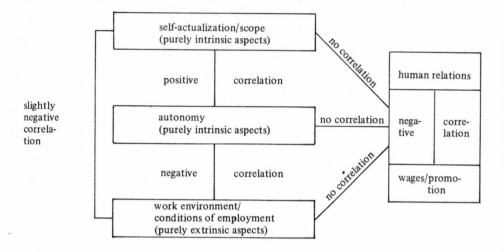

Considering the highly negative correlation between the extent to which purely extrinsic aspects on the one hand the extent to which human relations and wage/promotion aspects on the other are emphasized as work motives, four types of work orientation will frequently occur in actual practice:

— employees emphasizing the job itself and social contacts;
— employees emphasizing work environment/employment conditions and social contacts;
— employees emphasizing the job itself and pay/opportunities for advancement;
— employees emphasizing work environment/employment conditions and pay/opportunities for advancement.

(2) From the foregoing typification it follows, inter alia, that a job-aimed motivation and a motivation aimed at earning money need not — contrary to what is often heard — contradict each other. This holds also for an instrumental and intrinsic work orientation: one may be interested in the job itself and yet, for example, consider the work situation as a means to achieve goals outside the work environment; quitting the work organi-

sation therefore need not always mean that the reason of it is to be found within the work situation.

(3) The willingness-to-work concept is too rough to indicate the relation with satisfaction. A distinction should be made between a willingness relating to perform the work dictated by the present work situation (=involvement in present work position) and a willingness of a more general nature, that is to say, which — independently of the present work situation — relates rather to participation in the work process as such. Failure to make this distinction may offer an explanation for the mostly contradictory findings concerning the relation between work satisfaction and willingness to work. The more general willingness to work is, in fact, only slightly affected by the satisfaction with the present work situation. The willingness to work in the sense of involvement in present work position on the other hand is highly dependent on the extent of job satisfaction and, notably, on the satisfaction with the work itself.

Schematically the correlation between satisfaction and willingness to work could be outlined as follows:

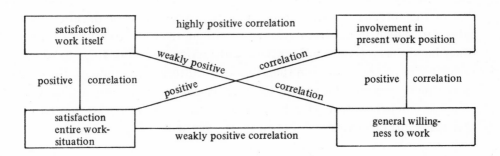

(4) The theory propounded by Herzberg c.s. that (a) aspects bringing about satisfaction cannot cause dissatisfaction and (b) intrinsic aspects are only satisfiers and extrinsic aspects are only dissatisfiers, does not hold. All aspect areas — purely intrinsic, purely extrinsic, human relations and wage/promotion aspects — may be sources of satisfaction as well as dissatisfaction. This is highly dependent on the nature of work orientation. If employees are involved mainly oriented to purely intrinsic aspects, the presence or the absence of these will cause satisfaction or

dissatisfaction, respectively; if, however, employees are involved mainly oriented to purely extrinsic aspects, then satisfaction/dissatisfaction will be created, principally due to the presence/absence of these aspects. The presence or absence of purely extrinsic and purely intrinsic aspects will, as regards their influence (direction and strength), on satisfaction/willingness to work not be different from each other, if the two aspect areas as work motives do not or hardly differ from each other in significance. In our investigations and in an investigation by Thierry (with unskilled and semi-skilled blue-collar workers) the foregoing applied, for example, to blue-collar workers who had received elementary education only.

Satisfaction or dissatisfaction are therefore not determined by the nature of the work orientation (NB intrinsically motivated employees are in principle not more satisfied than extrinsically motivated employees) or by the actual work situation, but by their coordination.

A policy aimed at raising the satisfaction and involvement in the present work position should take into account the motivation structure and pertinent differences between categories of employees.

(5) In general, the influence of the socio-cultural environment on the nature of the work orientation existing in the employees is greater than that of the actual work situation. The actual work situation or rather the extent to which it has been attuned to the motivation structure, on the other hand, has a greater influence on satisfaction and willingness to work in the relevant work situation than the socio-cultural environment. Insofar as the more general willingness to work is concerned — the willingness which is independent of what is dictated by the relevant work situation — the socio-cultural environment is more decisive again.

(6) As positional characteristics by which employees clearly differ from each other in motivation structure, social and company stratification, training level and age may be mentioned with regard to the accentuation of purely intrinsic and purely extrinsic aspects and marital status as characteristic with regard to the accentuation of wage/promotion aspects.

(7) Purely intrinsic and purely extrinsic aspects as work motives become more significant or less significant as employees (a) of a higher social and company stratification; (b) of a higher training level; (c) of lower age are involved.

Concerning training and stratification, it may be stated that both the values and criteria inherent in a certain stratification or training (=highly determined by former social environment) and the extent to which particular categories of needs have been fulfilled cause a differentiation between those of a high stratification and those of a low stratification and those who have received higher and lower education. The higher the stratification and/or training (former social environment), the more the employee himself is expected to consider the work-content as important (NB hence the progressive increase in general willingness to work as the level increases) and the work environment as unimportant. The higher the stratification or education (former social environment), the more the employee finds himself also in a position that he has sufficiently fulfilled socio-economic needs, the greater the chance that he will consider other aspects important (need for self-actualization, personality integration). Insofar as the age variable is concerned, it may be stated that younger people compared to older people have, in general, higher expectations, and have not yet adjusted their needs to what is actually feasible in the future and besides are faced with values and criteria accentuating success, achievement of ambitions, indiscrimination in work, taking risks, etc. Younger people are expected to try to prove themselves.

(8) That, on the one hand, blue-collar workers tend to place less emphasis on purely intrinsic aspects and more emphasis on purely extrinsic aspects than white-collar workers, does not imply that they are also more motivated by extrinsic than by intrinsic aspects. Blue-collar workers employed in the process industry consider aspects bearing on job content to be just as significant as or even more significant than aspects bearing on the work environment. This holds in particular for the junior staff.

(9) In addition to the training level the type of education, too, and in particular the influence of the former social environment, which manifests itself in this type of education, play a role in the accentuation of particular aspects as work motives. For example, a clear dividing line may be discerned in the accentuation of purely intrinsic and purely extrinsic aspects between primary and extended primary education (working classes up to lower middle classes) on the one hand, and secondary and college education (middle and higher classes) on the other.

Besides the difference existing in these two types of education and the corresponding difference in work orientation, the differentiation in (former) environmental values may be of importance to the present work orientation. In the category of workers who have received primary or extended primary education the clerical workers are more oriented towards the wage and promotion aspects than the technical staff. The meagre opportunity for promotion, notably in a technologically highly developed work organization such as the process industry and the strong accentuation of the success value notably by clerical employees is not alien to this. Finally, university education evidently stimulates such a job orientation that university-trained employees from the outset consider aspects bearing on the development of personality and self-actualization to be the most important. Even persons belonging to the same social and/or company stratification do not accentuate these aspects to such a degree.

(10) The stronger accentuation of the wage and promotion opportunity aspects by married (male) employees is obvious, because, from a financialconomic point of view, their needs are fulfilled to a lesser degree as compared to the single (male) employee.

(11) Positional characteristics (manifesting more or less the degree to which harmonization of work situation and motivation structure has or has not taken place to a sufficient degree) by which employees clearly differ from each other in job satisfaction and involvement in present work position are age and tenure. Positional characteristics − emphasizing the socio-cultural environment and/or the personality structure − resulting in differences between employees in satisfaction and involvement are marital status and trade union membership.

Insofar as age and tenure are concerned, it may be assumed that it is these two characteristics through which in certain respects a difference in harmonization of the work situation (possibilities given for fulfilment of needs) and motivation structure is reflected. Younger employees and those who have just entered employment have more expectations (are − as has been ascertained − more critical) in particular with regard to the work itself, they have adapted their needs to a lesser degree than older employees and those who have been longer with the company. Hence, younger employees and those who have just entered employment are less satisfied with and feel less involved in their present work situation than older employees and those who have been longer with the company.

(12) Concerning marital status, further investigation should demonstrate whether single (male) employees are less satisfied with/feel less involved in their present work and work situation due to their being single (less dependent position) and/or their personality structure (critical of any situation including marital status).

This holds also for trade union membership. Here, too, further investigation should determine whether non-trade unionists are less satisfied with/feel less involved in their work situation owing to their not being members of a trade union and/or their personality structure (negative attitude).

(13) The high satisfaction/involvement of wholly unskilled blue-collar workers with their present work situation is characteristic. The reference frame of this category, (a) within the work situation − the process industry − for the most part skilled blue-collar and highly skilled whitecollar workers, (b) outside the work situation, their colleagues in dirty and assembly-line work, and the fact that on account of the level of technical training (requirement of certificates, more training) one cannot afford to be dissatisfied, may serve as an explanation. The fact that the four motivation structure factors within this category do practically not differ demonstrate that these employees look upon their work and their work situation as instrumental rather than as a goal in itself. This, too, may promote great satisfaction.

(14) The low satisfaction and involvement of university-trained employees may be caused by this category's critical attitude, the lower dependence on the work organization concerned, the smaller degree of willingness to adapt requirements for the fulfilment of particular needs and, probably, the policy which is still too much directed towards creating and/or maintaining a work situation attuned to the motivation structure of workers and salaried employees.

THE MULTINATIONAL ENTERPRISE IN THE FUTURE

John Leslie-Miller
Council of the Dutch T.U.C.
Den Haag, Netherlands

Prof. Perlmutter, lecturing Finance and Commerce at Pennsylvania University, has forecasted that by 1985 industry will be dominated by three hundred gigantic multinational enterprises. These giants will have a key position in the world's industry. He has tested his thesis on its value with thousands of businessmen, politicians and scientists. In the development between now and 1985, when the concentration will be completed, he distinguishes *three clearly overlapping phases.* As regards the number of 300 multinational enterprises mentioned before, Perlmutter assumes that it is very well possible that the world's economy in 1985 will only have room for fewer, say 200 of these giants.
I would like to say a few words now about the three phases from Perlmutter's thesis.

Phase 1

In this phase the concentration takes place on a national level. It includes the starting of the „Industrial Reorganization Corporation". We recognize this phase, for instance, in Great Britain in the foundation of British Leyland Corporation. It may be useful to say a few words about this practical example of national concentration.

For a considerable time business in the British motorcar industry had been on the wrong way, and especially the Morris and Austin Works worked with heavy losses. Under the pressure of the British Government a fusion was then realized between Leyland, the motor factory for tractors and lorries, and Austin and Morris. This much bigger organisation has succeeded in growing from a corporation that suffered heavy losses into one that makes reasonable profits. The example of the

British Leyland Corporation has been followed by the French, the Germans and the Japanese.

This phase of national mergers runs, roughly speaking, from 1968 until 1975. It is clear that the Netherlands, too, are still in this phase. But I already said that the phases overlap each other.

In other words, parts of phase 1 will be found back in phase 2 and parts of phase 2 have already begun in phase 1.

Phase 2.

This is the phase of the binational and trinational giant enterprises. The beginning of it has already manifested itself. There has e.g. been the Dunlop/Pirelli merger, followed by many others of the same kind between international and national concerns. Here are some examples: Mitsubishi/Philips, Rhone Poulenc/Bayer, Nestle/Unilever, etc.. The merging of these enterprises can be characterized as the „courtship period".

According to Perlmutter the essence of a binational or trinational enterprise is that „it controls a worldwide operation from more than one centre".

The British/Dutch enterprises Shell and Unilever have been operating in this way for a considerable time. At the end of the seventies there will be enterprises which will try to abandon the idea of central point and periphery. They will then have a form of organization that is equivalent to that which GMC is already aiming at now. General Motors is removing its Oldsmobile Division Works from Detroit and transferring it to England. This concept of binational and trinational mergers is based on the following interaction of factors.

(1) International enterprises are more and more realizing how thinly their overseas interests are spread. A great many American, European and Japanese enterprises are scarcely represented abroad and they will encounter difficulties in realizing new overseas establishments.

(2) The Factor of the „defi japonais" (Japanese challenge). Although Perlmutter does not share Herman Kahn's view that Japan will become a super-power in due course, he is convinced that European/Japanese or American/Japanese mergers will have to take place. According to his line of thought they will not only be realized as a consequence of a defensive strategy on the part of the Western enterprises, but also because Japanese concerns have the strong desire to expand in Europe and in the United States of America. The game is very simple! The industrial giant of the future must be represented at three places and these places are Europe, the United States of America and Japan. The big enterprises of the eighties will be strongly represented in these three parts of the world. A Fiat-British Leyland merger will not be enough for Agnelli (president of Fiat), it would be much better for him to merge with Honda instead of with Leyland.

Perlmutter also includes the Communist block of countries into his theory of bi- or trinationalism. He foretells that, at the end of the seventies, there will be binational enterprises having their central point behind the Iron Curtain and he sees the possibility of what he calls 'transideological offshoots to the other side', so, for instance, Fiat with an important Russian participation. Phase 2 runs till the beginning of 1980, being followed by phase 3.

Phase 3

This phase will be marked by multinational enterprises having multi-national Management Boards and multinational stock capital. The entire stock will then be deposited with the World Bank or with the United Nations. These enterprises will each have more than 1 million employees and an annual turnover of approximately 165 000 million dollars. What will become of the small organizations? What role will then be played by these small organizations? In Perlmutter's opinion they will remain profitable. It is the medium-size enterprises which will disappear. They will be taken over by the giant organisations or they will try to find parts of the world where the giants cannot find them. From there they will wage a kind of guerilla war against the big ones. Conspiracies and urging others to conspire will be quite common. Then there will be the role played by the sovereign state. World-wide organizations will be accepted by them as 'quasi political' institutes: Henry Ford (or his successors) will then lunch a bit more frequently with prime ministers. All world-wide organizations, especially those which operate in the Communist countries, will be characterized by full or partial participation of the governments. All kinds of appeals will be made to those universal organizations, not only by shareholders, but also by customers, such as social groupings, trade unions, politicians, etc.. Anticipating this development Prof. Perlmutter sees a social accounting system which can be used by the enterprises to demonstrate their good conduct, for instance, as far as the fight against air pollution or assistance to development countries is concerned.

Perlmutter, like all good prognosticians, remains somewhat reserved with regard to his own prognoses. In his opinion it does not matter so much what will exactly happen. What *is* important is what people will think will happen. And if they think so, they will see to it that it happens.

The position of the higher personnel

We shall have to take the picture described here into account, if we want to examine more closely the personnel policy with regard to more highly qualified staff. The place of the higher personnel in the mammoth organization of tomorow is distinctly different from that of higher personnel in the medium-sized enterprise of yesterday. While a member of that level was more or less identical with the owner/manager of an enterprise in the past, he will to a much greater extent merely be an employee in the giant organisation of tomorrow. He will be a salaried functionary and will just hold a position. In doing so he will be just as vulnerable as all other employees in former times. The institution of 'collective agreement' which was made compulsory by law in the Netherlands in 1927 is not applicable to higher personnel. The Committee for the study of Labour Conditions of the Centre for Higher Personnel of the NVV (The largest federation of Dutch Trade Unions, comparable to the TUC in Great Britain) realized this when it started its activities in 1968. In order to assist this category of workers — the executive staff of business organizations and public bodies — it has made some suggestions for individual labour contracts for employees who do not come under the collective agreement. This brochure is especially for young graduates who finished their study from the sector of tertiary education (scientific education and higher vocational training). 2500 unemployed university-trained people in the Netherlands will certainly increase the interest for this brochure. It may be useful to review some points of the brochure. For this purpose we shall have a look at three sections:

Work for third parties

In a number of cases it is considered necessary to insert a stipulation into a labour agreement against the carrying out of work for third parties against payment. This always entails a risk of restricting the employee's liberty. For that reason we would not advocate the insertion of such a clause into an individual labour contract.

Competitive condition

It is sometimes a habit of the employers to bind the medium grade and higher personnel by means of a competitive condition. The legislator has already taken a number of measures in this matter. (Article 1637 of the Civil Code).

We would point out that, in principle, such a condition should be rejected, because it often has the consequence that the mobility of the employee, being the weaker party economically, is restricted. Only in very few cases is the little protection against unfair competition by means of this condition of any real value to the employer. Neither modern technology nor modern methods of market analysis and marketing can be kept outside the enterprise through the stipulations of a competitive condition. Although the judge has the right of mitigation, the competitive condition often means that the person concerned has to build up an entirely new career, which is particularly difficult for employees in the middle groups, and certainly for higher personnel, especially of the older age groups.

If a provision imposing a restraint has to be accepted in the labour agreement all the same, it should at least be restricted to a reasonable period of time; any penalty should be well-defined and not too heavy. Moreover, it should be clearly stated that a provision imposing a restraint can only be valid, if the employee submits his resignation at his own initiative, or is dismissed for serious reasons and further if it can be proved that the interests of the employer are harmed by the activities of the dismissed employee.

During the period in which a provision imposing a restraint is applied, the employee in question should go on receiving his salary. In this connection mention must be made of the risk that — however favourable such a stipulation in restraint may be — the judge will easily tend to declare the provision applicable in such a situation, without making use of his right of mitigation.

This causes particular problems, especially for technical staff who lose their practical knowledge during such a period of compulsory inactivity and cannot follow new technical developments sufficiently, and also for commercial personnel who would lose important business relations, when they can no longer maintain personal contacts.

Job description and salary

It is of eminent importance with respect to this question that one aims at obtaining at least a clear and objective description of the job and of the organizational system in which the functionary in question is employed. From this the content and extent of the function of the person concerned and his competence may appear, but also his place in the hierarchic and communication pattern of the enterprise.

Now it should be observed that even with an extensive job description all sorts of questions may still arise, because in addition to official patterns of communication and competence of decision making there are also a number of informal relations which exercise an appreciable influence on the relationships within the enterprise.

The latter relationships cannot be formulated, yet, stating the formal situation already means a great deal. It is justified to have the job description rewritten every time when the content of the function has changed.

Maintaining a job description made at the beginning of one's employment and not adapting it to the changing conditions gives rise to difficulties. It is evident that the person concerned wishes to have the modifications of the job description made in writing.

These were some of the points from the suggestions made by the committee.

Conclusion

Finally I would like to make the following remarks:

(1) Being a member of one of the trade unions is still something considered as not being proper for higher personnel. Therefore, the functionaries in question are apt to join some group organization. While the motive to do so was quite clear in former days — when the higher personnel identified themselves with their employer — this motive will no longer play any part in the world of to-morow, the world of the multinationals. It is clear that an individual labour contract only makes sense if one can appeal to it. Legal advice by specialized lawyers can then be of the greatest importance. Only an individual member of the higher personnel may often not find the right way. However, if he is a member of one of the trade unions, he may appeal to the best specialists in this field.

In this connection the factor of power, of course, plays a part. It is evident that the authority of the official trade unions with more than one million members is greater than that of the dwarf organizations, which call themselves professional or group organizations. It is because of this authority that it is possible for the big unions to organize themselves in such a way that their assistance to members is not only rhetorical, but real.

(2) For the manager of a new enterprise which forms part of the multinational, the situation has clearly changed.

164

Fig. 1 Roles of Chief Executives[1].

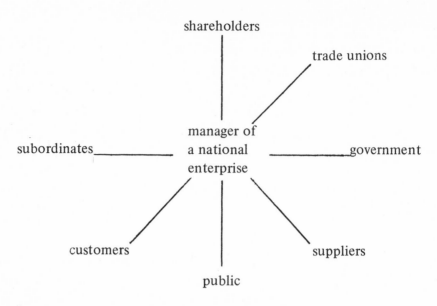

I. Role played by the manager of a national enterprise.

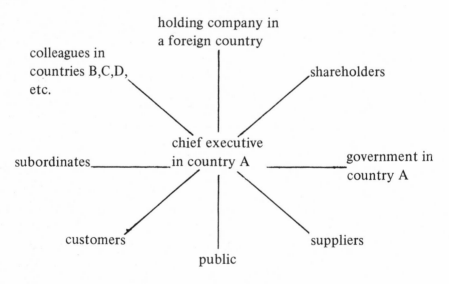

II. Role played by the chief executive of a daughter company abroad (A)[1].

1) From R. Dahrendorf, Essays in the Theory of Society, Routledge (1968) chapter 2.

If we compare the role played by the manager of a national enterprise with that played by the chief executive of a multinational firm we get the scheme of Fig. 1.

From role II of the chief executive it appears that this functionary's task is made more comprehensive and more responsible by operations which reach over the frontiers of countries. If he gets into a conflict situation, it is because he has often to play different and sometimes inconsistent roles simultaneously.

This situation is made still more difficult by the fact that superiors, sub-ordinates, customers, suppliers and colleagues are often of different nationalities.

Moreover, it is clear that the field of strategic decisions lies outside the chief executive's field of view. He is no more than the 'chief executive' i.e. the person who carries out a policy which is fixed by others at a distant part of the world.

Here we have the essential difference between a national manager and the chief executive of a multinational enterprise. In the former case the fields of strategic and routine decisions are integrated. In the latter, however, these domains are separated.

This means at the same time that the legal position of the chief executive has become just as uncertain as the legal position of the executive personnel, employed by a multinational enterprise.

POSSIBILITIES AND LIMITS OF PROBLEM SOLVING
IN INDUSTRIAL POLLUTION

Manfred Fischer
Institut für Systemtechnik und Innovationsforschung
Karlsruhe, Federal Republic of Germany

Material and energetical wastes have always been and will always be a problem of the production process. Even if they are not considered as pollutants — sometimes heavily emitting stacks were a sign of industrial well being — they give rise to extra costs: raw materials have to be refined, waste water has to be transported to the next river or lake, waste heat means decreased efficiency.

The most obvious way to reduce these costs is to use natural dissipation processes for the disposal of gaseous, dissolved or solid waste. By dissipation we mean the processes of dilution, chemical break down, sedimentation etc. which all tend to decrease the amount of noxious waste immission present in that part of the biosphere which is the habitat of man. It should be clear to all of us that the rate of dissipation is beyond human control and that the human habitat already covers most of the usable land. Therefore, the rate of emission must be kept below the rate of dissipation.

The rate of emission (in tons per year) is equal to the production (equally in tons per year) times a technical parameter, the specific emission. Table 1 shows some examples from the literature. There are two principle ways of reducing the specific emission of some given material: to use it in a recycling process or as a byproduct or to change it into some other material which can be either discharged into the biosphere or completely sealed up. Let us consider the case of sulphur in fossil fuels. The sulphur oxide which can be removed from the stack gases can either be changed into sulphuric acid and sold or it can be disposed of as gypsum in the sea or on the moon say.

Table 1: Types and Rates of Emission.

Product	Process	Raw material	Waste	Sec. Emission (related to the output)	Reference
Electrical Energy	Thermal power station	Oil	SO_2	3.68 kg SO_2/Gcal	Bergmann − Krämer[5]
"	"	Natural gas	-"-	8.10 kgSO_2/Gcal	
H_2SO_4	Catalytic Process	Sulphur	-"-	0.5 %	
Paper	Paper Mill	Wood	organically polluted water	waste water 10−300 l/kg BRD: ∼ 30g/kg paper	
Hydrocarbons	Raffinery	Raw oil	Hydrocarbons	1−0.1 %	Reine Luft für morgen[6]

We will now consider some problems luring on the way to perfect pollution control.

Economical and social problems

Today, as a rule of thumb, the German industry uses 6%-10% of its investment for pollution control, 10% actually holds for the chemical industry[1]. In general this poses no economic problem. In some industries, however, the financial burden would have to be much higher, the paper mills have a sale of 4,50 DM/t water used and total water costs of about 2 DM/t. If the tendency to place more and bigger plants (of 10^6 t/year capacity) in densely crowded areas proceeds, the marginal cost for further reduction of the specific emission may start to rise exponentially. This will stop the concentration process, thus limiting the growth of the industrial regions.

One of the basic structural dilemmas is commonly referred to as the tragedy of the commons. It is due to the fact that the public and the politicians assess the actual benefits of material growth more easily than the future drawbacks from pollution. The legislation necessary to enforce better pollution control therefore proceeds very slowly and government is often unable to stop the continuous degradation of the biosphere. Furthermore, part of the immission is often due to the emissions in other countries which cannot be controlled by the national government. International action is difficult to accomplish because all behave according to the principle: ,,I keep my country clean and tip the waste in neighbourland.''

The MIT-group of Meadows et al. used it's world model for 'long-term technology assessment'[2]. They found that recycling had the counter-intuitive effect of stimulating further industrial growth thus sharpening the ecological crisis. However, it is difficult to see how this can be consistent with the mass balance; if part of the waste is recycled pollution has to go down.

One can reduce pollution from production and consumption by increasing the lifetime of products. This would induce a shift of labor force from production to services[3]. The social consequences of this process should be carefully assessed. The productivity of service work, for example, is lower and the training of the worker must be improved. Also the emission from many small service plants is more difficult to control than that of one big production plant.

Technological Problems

Bartocha (loc.cit.) indicates a lot of interesting technological alternatives mainly in the field of what is called „umweltfreundliche Technik" in German (low waste technology). In this short note I would like to consider the problem of sealed-up disposal of waste. There will always be an appreciable amount of solid waste which has to be kept out of the hydrosphere and atmosphere: compounds of the heavy metals, of arsen, long lived radioactive material etc. If all sulphur were to be removed from the fossil fuels currently in use, we would produce three times as much sulphur as is needed thus creating a huge dumping problem. Sealing such wastes in cement and dumping them into the sea is certainly no solution. Dumping them into salt mines — which have been decoupled from the water cycle for geological time spans — is not generally possible due to the lack of salt mines. The space people have suggested to put these wastes into orbit using hydrogen powered rocket stages for the passage through the atmosphere — thus introducing no extra pollution from the combustion process. If it were possible to exploit extra terrestrial raw materials heavily polluting production processes could be performed outside the terrestrial biosphere. (Caution must be taken in order to avoid an increase of urban refusal). It seems from what has been said that the technological means for effective pollution control are at hand. Is the pollution crisis a 'no problem'?

Physical limits to growth

By 'growth' we mean growth of population, of habitable space and of income per capita. It has been the historical role of technology to push back the limits of such growth. Now it has been claimed that technology itself sets the limits for further growth by pollution and resource depletion. The MIT study is only the most sophisticated and advanced attempt to prove this thesis and to calculate the time left before reaching that limit. The thesis essentially states that the limit is imposed by natural laws and therefore it can not be exceeded by technological means. In order to prove the existence of such a limit one has to assume that an ideal technology is available, i.e. we will assume that material pollution is perfectly eliminated which will increase the energy use per unit of production. We are then left with thermal pollution only. By thermal pollution we describe the fact that all energy used on earth is finally radiated into outer space. On its way out it is heating the atmosphere. The natural temperature of the atmosphere is due to the balance between incoming radiation (the solar constant which is equal to $1400 \text{ MW}/\text{km}^2$, i.e. one big power station per km^2 (!)) and outgoing radiation, being proportional to the fourth power of the atmosphere's temperature[4]. Any extra energy used by man is equivalent to an increase of the solar energy thus rising the temperature of the atmosphere.

Meyer-Abich[5] concludes that an extra energy consumption of 1% of the solar constant could rise the mean temperature of the atmosphere by $1°C - 1,5°C$. In 1970 the total consumption of primary energy on earth corresponded to only 0,8‰ of the solar constant. However, locally this value may reach 10% and more. With the present possible rate, world energy production would reach 1% of the solar constant in roughly 100 years. The consequences are not yet foreseeable but may well be disastrous for many regions. This is one example where technology assessment is severely hampered by the lack of basic knowledge. Let us suppose that we knew that the temperature rise would not affect the human death rate. Clearly some generally accepted criterion for the determination of the maximum acceptable temperature increase or climate modification were necessary in order to assess the consequences of unlimited growth. Physical calculations are never sufficient to establish the limits to growth.

What are the prospects of limiting the excess energy consumption? Some major reductions could be made by improving the thermal insulation of buildings and by changing to collective transportation. The direct use of the solar energy or of geophysical sources (tides, wind, waterpower) should be increased although it is restricted to some limited regions.

Furthermore, if the energy consumption were 1% of the solar constant and the efficiency of the direct transformation of solar energy into electricity were 10% then 10% of the available land would be used for energy production (in the Federal Republic of Germany less than 10% of the land is now used for houses, industry and traffic).

Summing up we may say that an environmental crisis in the industrial countries — which already have a very low population increase — may be avoided if the organizational, financial and technological resources are consciously used and the energy consumption is limited to say 0,1% of the solar constant.

References:

1) Materialien zum Umweltprogramm der Bundesregierung 1971 — Drucksache VI/2710 des Deutschen Bundestages, Bonn (1971)
2) D.H. Meadows et al., The Limits to Growth, New York (1972) p. 137
3) H. Bartocha in: M.J. Cetron and C.A. Ralph, Industrial Application of Technological Forecasting, Wiley, New York (1971) p. 271
4) U.K. Hubbert, The Energy Resources of the Earth, Scientific Americany Sept. (1971) p. 61-70
5) B. Bergmann, and H. Krämer, Technischer und wirtschaftlicher Stand sowie Aussichten der Kernenergie in der Kraftwirtschaft der BRD, 1. Teil Jülich (1972)
6) Reine Luft für morgen, Editor: Minister für Arbeit, Gesundheit und Soziales des Landes Nordrhein-Westfalen, Düsseldorf (1972)

NEW WAYS AND CONCEPTS
FOR IMPROVING THE QUALITY OF FOOD

Jürgen Reichling
Botanisches Institut, Universität Heidelberg
Heidelberg, Federal Republic of Germany

In the past few years it has become more and more noticeable that public interest in the quality of our food has steadily increased. This question is of interest not only to the public but also to scientists, and it is a problem which frequently gives rise to controversy. As I have only a short time at my disposal to talk on this subject, I shall only deal here with a certain number of problems which at present exist. I should like to concentrate on crops, with special emphasis on two important factors which determine the quality of our food: pesticides and chemical fertilizers.

It would seem that the term 'quality' is not measurable scientifically. In fact it is still today a complex term as far as agriculture is concerned. There is much controversy and discussion about the meaning of 'quality'. Some people consider the criteria of quality to be e.g. size, weight, storage and marketing possibilities and above all the appearance of a product. Others maintain that although these factors have to be taken into consideration in assessing the quality of a product, it is more important to pay attention to the substances contained and their qualitative and quantative composition. Prof. Schuphan[1], for example, wrote: ,,The classification which often measures quality according to maximum size or weight can seldom be approved of and used by those concerned with research into quality." According to Schuphan, the term 'quality' should be subdivided into 'outer and inner quality' and should comply with the following criteria: Pleasing appearance, possibly also good transport and storage capacities, characteristic taste and aroma free of impurities, and above all criteria which affect our health.

In the future there will be a demand for great 'biological value' in fruit, vegetables and cereals. According to Schuphan, this term comprises the nutritive value of crops, their wholesomeness and their value as far as the preservation of man's health is concerned. These factors cannot be determined by the presence of a few chemical substances, but only by nutrition experiments. The term 'biological value' represents in general the sum of all chemicals contained which have a positive effect, whereby the negative ones limit the total effect of the final result. Both anorganic and organic components are taken into consideration, e.g. trace elements, essential oils, vitamins, minerals, sugar, fatty oils, protein and starch. These substances have a positive or negative effect on man's health and the interreaction is either neutral, synergistic or antagonistic.

I should now like to consider how various fertilization methods and the use of chemical pesticides can endanger the quality of our food and the possibilities which exist for reducing these dangers in the future, thereby improving the quality of our food.

For factors influencing the quality of crops (simplified) see the following Figure:

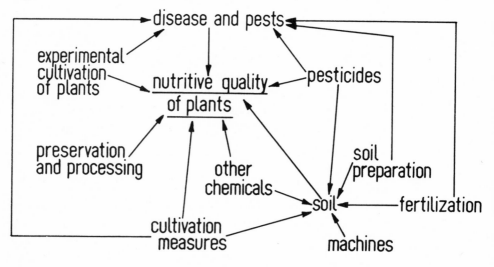

Obtaining the greatest yields possible and rationalization are the maxims of our agricultural system. These aims, however, can only be realized by means of the steadily increasing use of technical and chemical aids. Our cultivated soil therefore suffers from a lack of humus and the widespread and one-sided application of chemical fertilizers. This leads to the breaking down of the resistence of our plants to pests and disease, which in turn requires an even greater use of pesticides which are bad for the environment.

Chemical fertilizers and pesticides can lead to a decline in the quality of our crops and seriously endanger our health. For example, increasing quantities of chemical fertilizers can diminish the taste of a product and reduce the amount of valuable substances contained, it can also lead to poorer durability, exaggerated growth and excessive water content. There is also the danger of an increase in nitrate content in plants, which may be reduced to nitrite, the latter being especially harmful to babies.

Pesticide residues can reduce the quality of our food and endanger the health of the population. Contrary to the repeated assertions of interested parties that pesticides are not harmful, there are the following points to be considered:

1. Some pesticides recommended by the authorities have already proved to be mutagen and cancerogen, as for example Amitrol, Aramid and Thiourea which are cancerogen[2].

2. All over the world there is a noticeable growing resistence of pests to all kinds of pesticides. This forces one to use even more harmful chemicals and to produce alternative pesticides, often more dangerous than the first[3].

3. We know little about the physiological affects of pesticides and about changes in plants, animals and man himself due to these.

4. There has up to now been little research into chronic effects and late injury, nor into synergistic, cumulative and additive effects. It is, however, certain that these effects do exist with regard to pesticides[4].

5. The controls of harmful residues in our food have up to now been limited to a few samples selected at random. Usually complaints are not heard until after a product has been sold. This is no guarantee of protection for the consumer.

One possible way to overcome these difficulties and to improve the quality of our food is demonstrated by *integrated pest control*, combined with biological agricultural measures such as well-balanced fertilization, the right conditions of growth, e.g. soil and climate, and biological and ecological cultivation methods.

Integrated pest control is defined as a pest management system that, in the context of associated environment and the population dynamics of the pest species, utilizes all suitable techniques and methods in as compatible a manner as possible and maintains the pest populations at levels below those causing economic injury (FAO).

This broad definition, implying the fullest use of natural mortality factors complemented when necessary by artificial methods, needs no alteration. Integrated pest control is not synonymous with pest management, which is equivalent in most usage to the term pest control. It is recognized that chemicals will be an essential component of most integrated control programmes, the level of chemicals used and the timing of their application being based on ecological considerations and the supervision of the pest situation. Supervised control is therefore essential for many integrated control systems. One of the aims is to utilize chemicals efficiently by keeping usage to the minimum required for economic control and hence to minimize undesirable pesticide effects. Integrated pest control is based on biological and ecological considerations. It is, for example, well-known that the biotope is influenced by the entire complex of organisms, plants and animals present in cultivated crops, namely the pests, their natural enemies, their competitors, the other inhabitants of the same biotope and their food, together with weeds and other wild plants other than the crop itself, the soil and its care, cultivation and preparation techniques, general physical conditions dependent on climate and weather and, above all, occasional or permanent human activities[5]. Ths type of unity is referred to as an ecosystem.

The aim of integrated pest control is to maintain the ecological balance in a cultivated area by means of suitable measures. Therefore it is necessary to do more than only to integrate chemical and biological methods into the final form desired. All methods of cultivation and crop protection must be practised according to ecological considerations aimed at keeping pests down to an economically unimportant level.

As has already been mentioned, integrated pest control makes use of all biotic and abiotic limitations, whereby the term 'biotic limitation' in integrated pest control is usually purposely used in its widest sense, denoting every activity of carnivorous small and large animals and also the effect of parasites or morbiferous agents which are capable of lowering the average incidence of another living organism, especially the pest in question.

Unfortunately we know too little still about the limiting factors which would be able to keep the pests to a minimum. Furthermore, pesticides and methods of soil cultivation have a great influence on the growth of the pest population. Let us remember e.g. the dangers of the aquirement of resistence and the changing importance of specific kinds of pests. The wrong kind of fertilization can lead to plants becoming more prone to disease and more susceptible to insects.

The methods of integrated pest control enable a drastic reduction of the use of pesticides to take place, as proved by H. Steiner, R. F. Smith and others in the cultivation of apples and cotton[6].

The methods are continuously being improved and used for other plants also, e.g. for vegetables and peaches. Integrated pest control aims eventually to prevent an increase in the number of pests and diseases by taking into consideration ecological factors in a cultivated area.

This goal can only be reached with the aid of suitable fertilization and cultivation measures. It is possible, for example, to strengthen the resistance of plants by means of well-balanced fertilization, to counteract the lack of humus, to prevent soil erosion and improve the quality of crops. Furthermore, increased nitrate content in tissue can be prevented. Well-balanced fertilization includes all measures aiming at this goal, such as the use of waste compost, leguminose (nitrogenizers), composted animal dung and stable manure, fertilization using plants themselves, trace elements and the therapeutic use of chemical fertilizers.

'Balanced fertilization' has the following positive influences on soil, plants and landscape:

The Influence of Balanced Fertilization on Biological Factors

Soil	Plants	Landscape
a) Preservation of soil fertility and of the physical soil structure	a) resistence to pests and disease	a) reduction of erosion
	b) high quality and physiological nutritive value	b) protective plant covering
b) productive capacity		
		c) no strain on water conservation
c) no soil compression	c) healthy growth	
d) no oversalting		

The combination of balanced fertilization, ecologically determined cultivation methods and integrated pestcontrol promises to contribute positively towards solving the many biological and nutrition problems in the future.

The new ways to improve quality cannot be considered as a small correction of the existing agricultural methods; it means the introduction of a completely new agricultural structure. There have been enough initial attempts to introduce biological methods into agriculture. In the developing countries also[7], only biological measures can survive in the long run. The demand for better quality food is even more important in these countries, as not only calories but also protein and vitamins are an essential part of man's diet.

The realization of a completely new agricultural structure is, however, not only a scientific and technological problem, but also a socio-political one. It is only when changes in the form of agricultural competition occur, that we can hope to save agriculture from disaster.

179

References

1) W. Schuphan, Zur Qualität der Nahrungspflanzen, BLV Verlagsgesellschaft, München, Bonn, Wien (1961)

2) R. Preussmann, Der Einfluß von Umweltfaktoren auf die Krebsentstehung Evangelische Akademie Rheinland-Westfalen, Ökologisches Informationsseminar II (1971)

3) FAO, Report of the FAO Conference on Pesticides in Agriculture, Meeting Report, No.PI/162/17/
FAO, Reports of the second to seventh session of the FAO Working Parties of Experts on Resistance of Pests to Pesticides, held in Rome, 1966-1971, namely PI/1966/M/13, PI/1967/M/18, PI/1968/M/10, PI/1969/M/17, AGP/1970/M/9, AGP/1971/M/7

4) G. Krampitz, Pestizidrückstände im Stoffwechsel der Warmblüter, Hohenheimer Arbeiten 61, Allgemeine Reihe, Eugen Ulmer Verlag (1972)

5) H. Heddergott, The Principles of Integrated Pest Conrol, Report on the Seminar: Recent Developments in the Field of Plant Protection and Pest Control, 1969, DOK 458 A/a/S9/69

6) R.F. Smith, Effects of Manpulation of Cotton Agro-Ecosystems on Insect Pest Populations, Presentation at the Conference on the Ecological Aspects of International Development in Virginia (1968)
R.F. Smith, Patterns of Crop Protection in Cotton Ecosystems, Talk given at Cotton Symposium on Insect and Mite Control and Research in California (1969)
H. Steiner, Integrierter Pflanzenschutz im Obstbau, (Qualitas Plantarum Et Materia Vegetabiles, Volumen XV (1967)
H. Steiner, Plant Protection with and without Risks, Report of the Intern. Conference on New Trends in Plant Protection, EPPO Bulletin No.1, Paris (1971)

7) K. Egger, J. Reichling, et al., Ökologische Probleme ausgewählter Entwicklungsländer, erstellt im Auftrag des Bundesministeriums für wirtschaftliche Zusammenarbeit, Heidelberg (1972), Verlag Buske, Hamburg (1973)

Assessing the Distribution, Application and Consumption of New Technologies

ASSESSING SOCIAL AND ECONOMIC IMPACTS

Robert H. Rea
Abt Associates, Inc.
Cambridge, Massachusetts, USA

Before discussing the details of an example of an impact analysis, it is important to report on the recent history of our work in this area. We have conducted the following studies that focus on social and economic impact assessment. (In most cases, we were a part of an interdisciplinary team that included specialists in the physical, biological, and engineering sciences):

(1) About four years ago we made a forecast of the demand for the use of airport and seaport facilities in Boston. The forecast was compared with existing and planned facilities, and an assessment was made of the social and economic consequences of alternative methods of responding to the demand (or not).

(2) About two years ago we assessed the social consequences of the practices of a large multi-national firm for the developing nations that supplied its products.

(3) During the last year, we have conducted seven projects dealing with the social and economic consequences of engineering alternatives for problems of water supply, waste-water treatment, housing, and high-way construction.

In generalizing about these projects, one can say that the method of approach is straightforward, but the implementation is not.

Now let's put a little life into the fuzzy terms 'social and economic impact' by taking a specific example — the Boston water supply problem. Boston gets water from a large reservoir system in Western

Massachusetts. The water is being used faster than its reservoirs are being replenished. The Corps of Engineers has proposed three alternative solutions, one of which is to 'do nothing'.

Given this problem, the following steps were taken:

Step 1: Define impact categories (See Table 1)
Step 2: Develop baseline data (community profiles) for all communities involved in the same categories as shown in Table 1.
Step 3: Extrapolate baseline data — economic and residential activity — from 1970-2020. This time period was required by the 50 year life assumed for the projects.
Step 4: Estimate the changes from the baseline extrapolations induced by each of the engineering alternatives.

As can be imagined, this process is fraught with data availability problems, level of detail, mis-matches and extrapolation uncertainties.

Unfortunately, we cannot proceed to the following step of active public participation for the *valuation* of change and in the selection of alternatives because this project is scheduled for the more traditional public hearing process. But at least, the planners will be much better prepared to answer social and economic impact questions than they would have been without the study.

As you may have noticed, the impact estimates were made by the *proposers* of the projects — and they were made in a timely fashion so that the results did influence some engineering considerations. Although representatives of the affected areas were involved in the data collection process, they were not asked to anticipate any consequences or to evaluate them.

However, we are in the process of designing an experiment in *citizen participation*. Although the project is not yet approved, its concept is relevant. It addresses one of the major problems of citizen participation. One might normally expect the scenario to go something like: the Corps announces their plans to clean up the river and encourages citizen groups to comment on them. The groups develop a superficial position, based only on the uninformed self-interests of their constituency. This is neither good politics nor good science.

The project is to provide the financial resources that existing groups (and those that may form during the course of the work) feel that they need to inform themselves in their own way about the technical aspects of the project and their social, economic, and institutional implications. The objective is *not* to inform the people on the obvious wisdom of the proposed plans, but to encourage the widest possible solicitation of viewpoints on the plausible changes that would result from plan alternatives and an assessment of the 'goodness' and 'badness' of these changes. The solicitation of these viewpoints would be made at a stage in the project when the technical alternatives have been desribed at a level of detail that is adequate for the formulation of group inputs but when significant changes in the proposals are still possible. In fact, the alternative of not doing the project at all is still one of the options.

If this project is carried out, it would be one of the few occasions when all of the steps in the optimal technology assessment process would have been taken.

In general, all countries of the world must deal with strong forces advocating both exploitation and conservation of natural resources. The previous example shows one possible process of resolving the conflicts between these apparently opposing forces with the aid of a systematic process. The process is not new. It is the traditional design process of proposing alternatives, anticipating consequences, changing the alternatives, anticipating how the consequences will respond to the changes, and finally selecting the alternative that produces the most desirable set of consequences. The *new* parts are the need to consider a much broader range of consequences (environmental, social, economic) and the need to rely on a much larger number of people to identify and value them.

There are at least three compelling reasons for making this additional effort.

(1) It makes better technical plans — cheaper, more effective, longer lasting, if impact assessments are made an integral part of the design

Table 1: Socioeconomic impact measurement

Impact Categories	Suggested Measures	Units	Time Period
1. Land Use	Net change in the percent distribution of acres devoted to industrial, commercial, agricultural, residential, and recreational uses.	Percent	Long
	Net change in land use caused by the various physical diversion facilities (e.g., dams, pipelines, tunnels).	Acres	Short & Long
	Net change in the amount of land available for development.	Acres	Long
2. Population	Net changes in the age, income, race and ethnicity distributions of the local population, particularly in the donor areas.	Percent	Short & Long
3. Municipal Finance	Loss of assessed valuation as a percent of community total.	Percent	Long
	Increase in assessed valuation resulting from improved water service.	Dollars	Long
	Net change (gain/loss) in tax revenue resulting from improved water service.	Dollars	Short & Long
4. Commercial Activity	Net change over normal trends in gross wholesale and retail sales of those facilities affected by availability of water resources.	Dollars	Short & Long
	Net number of businesses located (displaced) by a facility.	Number	Short & Long
5. Housing	Net change (increase/decrease) in number of housing units by number of bedrooms by price (OR).	Number	Short
	As a percent of community's total stock in the receiver area.	Percent	Short

	Category	Description	Units	Term
6.	Education	Net change in amount of classroom and other educational space required for projected change in school-age population resulting from in- and out-migration.	Sq. Ft.	Short & Long
		Net changes in cost of teacher and other education staff required for projected change in school-age population resulting from in- and out-migration.	Dollars	Short & Long
		Net change in cost of providing school services because of changes in busing.	Dollars	Short
		Use of facilities for educational programs.	Day/Yr.	Short
7.	Leisure Opportunities	Net change in the total number of acres of parks and playgrounds in the Study Area.	Acres Visitor Days	Short & Long
		Net change in the extent to which planned recreation space meets American Society of Planning Officials planning standards relating types of space to population characteristics.	Percent	Short
8.	Cultural Opportunities	Total number of churches, historical sites or other cultural institutions taken.	Number	Short
		Cost of relocating churches, historical sites and other cultural institutions, minus compensating payments.	Dollars	Short
		Increase in locational amenities (e.g., improved site planning, additional parking, etc.,) as a result of relocation.	No. of Improvements	Short
9.	Transportation	Net change in travel time as a result of facilities from major residential areas to activity centers: health, commercial, recreation, employment, education, cultural.	Min./ Trip x Trips/ Day	Short

188

10.	Municipal Services	Net change in cost of providing water, sewerage, and garbage service and other municipal services.	Dollars	Short & Long
		Net change in residential insurance rates.	Percent	Long
11.	Security	Number of positive and negative statements about the opportunities for system failure, as revealed by a content analysis of local news media.	Number	Short & Long
12.	Community Image	Changes in property values adjacent to supply facilities	Dollars	Short & Long
		Number of positive and negative statements about the community as revealed by a content analysis of local news media.	Number	Short & Long
13.	Community Cohesiveness	Total number of community, regional, statewide and national groups taking a position (making a public statement) for or against the project.	Number	Short
14.	Citizen Involvement	Total number of community, regional, statewide and national groups involved in the planning of the project, times the level of their involvement, according to the following scale of increasing involvement: 1. Attendance at hearing; 2. citizen opportunity to critique plans at public meetings; 3. periodic workshop planning sessions with community representatives; 4. community advocate planner participated on equal basis with technical staff in all planning activities; 5. appointment of arbitrative hearing officer who makes final decision in case of dispute between community and Army Engineers.	Weighted No.	Short

No.	Category	Description	Unit	Term
15.	Institutional Involvement	Total number of jurisdictions involved in the totality of the construction process for a water supply facility.	Number	Short & Long
		Number of applications submitted to the M.D.C. for water supply service by cities and towns; disposition and frequency of refusal.	Number	Short & Long
16.	Economic Stability	Net change in income resulting from construction and related activities.	Dollars	Short & Long
		New increase in private investment.	Dollars	Short & Long
17.	Real Income	Net change in per capita income.	Dollars	Short & Long
		Net change in tax assessments.	Dollars	Short & Long
		Net change in regional net income.	Dollars	Short & Long
18.	Employment	Number and type of jobs created/lost.	Number	Short & Long
19.	Industrial Activity	Change (increase/decrease) in number of industrial establishments.	Number	Short & Long
		Change in productivity indices.	Dollars	Short & Long
20.	Agricultural Activity	Change (increase/decrease) in number of farm acres.	Number	Short & Long
		Change in production per acre.	Dollars	Short & Long

process at every step and the same level of detail — *not* if they are just added on to the end of the process to satisfy a requirement.

(2) It is required by law as a formal expression of concern for the physical, social and economic environment. (The National Environmental Protection Act of 1969 and Section 122 of the Rivers and Harbours Act)

(3) Because of the need to seek guidance from an increasingly aware and skeptical public.

There are consequences that may have been overlooked by even the best planners and designers, and certainly a wide variety of inputs is absolutely essential to know which impacts are good, which impacts are bad, and for whom. Participation by the public is a way to obtain reactions to alternative proposals — because planners can be surprised. Additional benefits are derived from the increased sensitivity and education obtained by various publics and public servants about different value systems and the difficulties of distinguishing good from bad.

Conveniently, these three reasons parallel the major components of the process:

(1) Identification of the categories and dimensions of change.

(2) Quantification of impacts for alternative plans, where one of the alternatives is the no-action baseline.

(3) Valuation of the impacts by different actor groups.

This last point brings up the issue of *timing. When* should the public be invited to participate? Obviously, it should be not too soon — not too late — but just right. If it's too soon, the public doesn't participate because they can't work with nebulous planning objectives. If it's too late, the public rightly feels that the situation is just another exercise in which they are 'heard' as a matter of form, but their opinions have no meaningful effect on an already immutable plan design. Then what is 'just right'? It seems to be a point when alternatives have been well-articulated, but they are not rigid, and preliminary impact assessments have been made for each in a form that permits trade-offs among their respective costs and benefits.

In conclusion, we can say that social and economic impact assessment is a straightforward process of developing a logic for and selecting relevant impact categories and some corresponding indicators for which data can be collected. An extrapolation is then made to forecast how these indicators will change during the lifetime of the proposed project for scenarios *without* the project and *with* the various project alternatives. Although one should be as comprehensive as possible, within available time and resource constraints, it is not necessary to wait until everyone involved agrees with the categories, indicators and forecasts before an alternative can be recommended. For most projects, this time would never come. Project planners *should not* be expected to have anticipated *all* of the consequences of their proposals nor should they believe that they could. They *should* be expected to consider a wide variety of possible impacts and to present their expectations to as many people and groups that might be affected by the project as possible. Such a process, coupled with a political process for final selection of alternatives, would result in a situation where every reasonable effort had been made in project planning and where the responsibility for future unanticipated consequences was shared by those people who helped decide to go ahead.

Many problems remain. Some of the major issues are:

(1) *Presentation of information.* Where there are several technical plan alternatives and on the order of 20 categories of social and economic impact with several indicators in each category, it is very difficult for anyone to 'sum-up' the advantages and disadvantages so that a choice of alternative can be recommended. The application of a formal benefit-cost analysis suffers from oversimplification. Perhaps a system for establishing thresholds of each impact category, both alone and in combination with others, would be a useful development.

(2) *The development of informed groups.* Each project will require careful planning to promote the participation of existing groups and

those that may form during the course of the project that are 'representative'. These groups will undoubtedly require additional resources to inform themselves about the project alternatives before developing their points of view and to convince themselves that their information sources are independent and objective. Every effort must be made to guard against the 'establishment' image that is created where the agency proposing the project defines all of the alternatives (carefully designed so that a single pre-selected plan is obviously the 'best') and provides all of the information.

(3) *Final decision-making via a representative process.* Meaningful participation cannot be maintained unless the participants feel that there is some means for their views to be heard in a situation where they have some influence. In the case of the Merrimack example, the final decision to go ahead with the project will be made by the Public Works Committee of the U.S. House of Representatives. The members of this committee are elected representatives that can be influenced by the voters in their constituencies. Other mechanisms are possible, but the current practice of holding a single meeting where the public is 'heard' before the agency makes the decision is neither convincing nor equitable.

(4) *Time.* Unfortunately, project initiation will undoubtedly be delayed by a meaningful process of impact assessment and the selection of an alternative. Although problem solutions are always urgent, the process of solving them *must* be of equal urgency.

Although the process described by this paper may seem a bit idealistic, work is now in progress that can turn it into a reality. However, much more effort is needed before widespread diffusion can be achieved. I urge you to make it; I'm convinced it's worth it.

SOCIAL COSTS AND BENEFITS OF URBAN DEVELOPMENT

Paul Drewe
Netherlands Economic Institute
Rotterdam, The Netherlands

1. The Urban-Regional Context

Societies tend to a polarized development, polarized between (changing) core and peripheral areas. This development depends on the spatial impact of basic processes of urbanization or modernization such as emergence and diffusion of (technical and other) innovations, political control of decisions, migration of population, and (capital) investments[1]. He who judges societal performance at the national level only, commits a fallacy of average. This fallacy of national average may extend to popular performance measures such as per capita GNP as well as to emerging social indicators as 'indicators of change in basic wellbeing' (OECD).

The development of society, in the first place, 'happens' in regions. Whether the performance of a nation is more than just the sum of the performances of its regional components, largely depends on the implementation of urban-regional development policies[2].

If we want to trace the impact of new technologies in an urban-regional context it may prove useful to distinguish different types of environment[3]:

- natural environment (including elements such as the airshed, quiet-and-noise zones and the like)
- spatial environment (e.g. airways space)
- transportation-utilities environment (ranging from commuting time to solid waste disposal)

— community-neighbourhood environment (including community characteristics such as densities and the services environment, judged by its
quality and nearness)
— microenvironments such as the household shelter (involving among
others household equipment) and workplaces (e.g. safety)

Quality of life depends on what is offered in each of these environments. That is why tracing the impact of new technologies on the
environment alone will not do. Sooner or later we have to assess
whether new technologies are doing 'good' or 'harm' to the quality of life.
life.

2. The Traditional Approach to Assessment

Traditionally, assessment problems are tackled by applying the criterion
of allocational or Pareto efficiency. A new technology will be judged to
be efficient if its adoption makes some users better off without reducing the welfare of anyone else, with welfare being measured in terms
of money or real income. A new freeway system, for example, will be
implemented, provided its aggregate monetary benefits to users (caused
by shorter travel times) exceed the monetary costs of constructing and
maintaining the system.
Although being 'allocationally efficient', an implementation of the new
freeway may nevertheless be deficient in two important ways. First,
monetary costs and benefits may have to be weighted differently for
different social groups, delinated primarily by social status (income,
education, occupation) and position in the life-cycle (age, family status,
household size). Second, allocational efficiency, as sketched above, does
not account for 'externalities' not all of which can be easily translated
into monetary terms and some of which cannot be expressed in money at
all. Users of freeways, for example, inflict costs on other users (through
congestion) as well as on non-users (through destruction and modification
of the physical environment, noise etc.). These are costs which, traditionally, have not been incorporated in attempts of assessment. Complexity
is added when one considers variations of 'weights' and 'externalities' over
time.

Both deficiencies, neglect of distributional efficiency and externalities, have led to emerging departures from the traditional approach. But the latter, by and large, is still 'in power'. Predominance of allocational efficiency has been favoured by operational advantages and by political support, while the adoption of new directions in assessment has been seriously hampered by measurement and policy obstacles.

3. Distributional Efficiency

With regard to distributional efficiency (which is the first meaning of 'social' as we understand it here) we need to disaggregate monetary costs and benefits according to social groups and over time. This is an intricate task as we cannot confine ourselves to primary and lower level effects of the technology in question. Changing the supply of transportation services in a given urban area, for example, does not only affect the transportation-utilities environment in the same area. Repercussions will be felt in other environments in the area as well, in the natural, spatial and community-neighborhood environment and to some extent in microenvironments, too. Besides, effects may spill over to other areas and even up the spatial hierarchy. Both indirect and higher level repercussions once again tend to 'discriminate' between population groups. All this asks for theories of urban systems. The most advanced modelling attempts, so far, can be classified as 'activity-location models'. These are models trying to 'locate' employment and population, starting from a given supply of stocks, 'adapted-spaces' and 'channel-spaces' including transportation infrastructure[4]. Model development in this field has received major impulses from Lowry's 'Model of Metropolis', developed around 1964 for Pittsburgh[5]. First, there were further developments in the United States before this line of research reached its actual boom in Britain[6]. Research efforts in Britain (until december 1971) have resulted in five operational models both at the sub-regional and at the town scale. Besides from that we also notice five major developments at a conceptual-experimental stage. Activity-allocation models of the Lowry type can be applied throughout the planning process: in analysis and understanding of the planning problem, at the stage of plan design and in evaluation of any proposed solution.

Representatives of the Lowry model heritage emphasize disaggregation and dynamization as priority targets for further research thus aiming at the empirical basis distributional efficiency asks for. Pursuing this line of research involves coping with the intricacy of the subject matter (in particular the complexity of lag-structures), with the statistical problem of estimating parameters on the basis of available data, and with the inadequacy of the data base itself. Simulation techniques may help to overcome these obstacles, at least to some extent[7]. We agree with Wilson et al. on that ,,Better theories of urban systems are needed, less aggregated, more explicitly dynamic and more related to our intuitive understanding of individual behaviour ... The general model (-to be aimed at-) ... is essentially a socio-economic spatial *behavioural* model of urban systems to measure impact" [8].

Suppose we would know present and future monetary costs and benefits approximatively and in a disaggregated manner, then we would be able to identify the impact of alternative changes in technology

— all satisfying the criterion of allocational efficiency
— all yielding the same aggregate values of monetary benefits and costs
— but each associated with a different cost-benefit distribution among social groups.

Thus an empirical basis would be provided for achieving distributional efficiency through political choice:
,,A system is efficient in the distributional sense if the distribution of real income between members of the system corresponds to the distribution desired by the planning or administrative agents. To achieve distributional efficiency it is necessary to tinker with prices in the system, either by subsidy or taxation"[9].

It may be considered as a high priority minimum requirement to identify at least the most disadvantaged groups of the population.

Solution of measurement problems alone will not do, if politicians are not willing to intervene and, vice versa, such an attitude encourages neither the development of better theories of urban systems nor their application to urban planning. Emerging concepts of social planning, related to citizen participation, stress that it is both necessary and feasible to turn the outcome of political decision-making into a 'dependent variable' instead of accepting it as given from outside the purely technical activity of urban-regional planning. As these views are closely connected with the social indicator movement we want to review them later on.

4. Social Indicators

Moving to externalities, we are going to deal with the second meaning of 'social' (costs and benefits). As far as these non-economic yardsticks of societal performance (known as 'social indicators') are concerned, we encounter similar proplems to those attached to distributional efficiency. But there is also the overriding new problem of what we should strive for, if not for maximum per capita GNP, and of handling benefits and costs which cannot (easily) be expressed in dollars and cents.

'Social costs' have been defined „as the divergence between the private costs borne by a firm or individual entrepreneur and the costs to others, or to the community which such individuals generate, but do not bear" (Bell). These costs, so far, have not been subtracted from established measures of society performance. Of course, social costs of private and public enterprise do not tell the full story of inadequacies of GNP as an indicator of welfare. Social costs of consumption exist as well as a look at the 'materials balance'[10] unmistakably shows. On the other hand, an account of society's importance for men should include social benefits, too. The movement toward „social reporting or its virtual synonyms: social indicators, social accounting, social intelligence" (Duncan) has started in the United States. The Johnson administration has even left a first trial of a social report behind, trying to measure the performance of the American society not only in terms of per capita GNP[11]. A wider range of goals has already been formulated for the regional level by Perloff[12]. The social indicator movement owes a major impetus to the Report for the Club of Rome Project, an alarming trend extrapolation which demonstrates the 'limits to growth' and even to human existence on a world scale: if things go on like they used to.[13]. Recently OECD, to quote only one venture, has started a social indicator program. It deserves special attention because OECD for quite some time has acted as a multinational pacemaker in the field of yardsticks for national 'progress'. Most of OECD's policy recommendations, however, have been predominantly growth-oriented. Now the OECD Council at Ministerial Level has determined „to devote more attention to how the extra wealth which the growth process creates may be better directed to improvements of the quality of life and the meeting of social aspirations" [14]. The social indicator program starts with a selection and definition of social concerns to be followed by the development of statistical indicators. Work is envisaged covering seven areas of social concern:

1. personal health and safety
2. personal development and intellectual and cultural enrichment through learning
3. occupational development and satisfaction
4. time and leisure
5. command over goods and services
6. the physical environment
7. the social environment[15].

5. Measurement Problems

As far as actual achievements in the field of social indicators are concerned, they are not too impressing yet. Plessas and Fein, evaluating the state-of-the art, have concluded that „.... the field is characterized by a great deal of peripheral verbosity" [16]. Measurement problems, no doubt, are tremendous. If one defines social indicators as 'indicators of change in basic well-being' one really has to cope with, what Gross has called, the 'mysteries of interest-satisfaction' or „all that philosophers have referred to as 'happiness'. It includes the disembodied satisfactions dealt with by economists and mathematicians under the name of welfare, benefits, utility, utiles, or (in the hard language of game theorists) 'pay offs' " [17].

Practitioners, however, need down to earth concepts, usually „a wide variety of 'surrogates', that is, indirect indicators that serve us as

quantitative substitutes or representatives" of satisfactions and dissatisfactions (Gross).

We want to discuss some of these surrogates, at least the most important ones, namely:

1. political statements and professional standards on the politicians' and
   planners' side and on the 'clients' side
2. real world choices made among various alternatives
3. monetary payments for services and goods that may be purchased
4. opinions expressed
5. allocation of time
6. gaming results.

Looking for social indicators we are not operating in a political-profes-
sional vacuum, of course. There are already relevant *political statements*
as well as *professional standards* which imply assumptions about basic
well-being or happiness of those for whom the planning is done. To
retrieve indicators from these sources is one possible strategy of
measurement. It asks for a specific logic of procedure as demonstrated
by Boyce (and others). „In order to analyze systematically the structure
and content of statements and criteria in urban planning, several major
metropolitan land use and transportation planning programmes were
selected for examination" [18]. This should be a critical examination as
implicit assumptions about interest-satisfaction of clients must be
checked against indicators originating from the clients themselves. With
regard to political statements this touches upon the question of political
representation which will be dealt with later when we are going to
discuss the political side of social indicators. As far as professional
standards are concerned, we cannot take them for granted either.
Empirical studies have shown that architect-planners tend to disagree
with clients, for example, on ratings of neigborhood quality. Disagree-
ment, however, may decrease with increasing educational level of
clients[19].

Moving to clients as a source of social indicators, we need at least a
simple behavioural model to evaluate the pros and cons of the remaining
five surrogates mentioned above. Behaviour (b) can be assumed to be
determined by a mix of choice and constraint. Choice refers to interest
or preference (p), the component useful as a social indicator. Constraint

refers to both actors and their environment, or to put it in another way, constraint has a demand- and a supply-side. Demand-constraints (c^d) rise from the fact that actors' reaction potential is limited by factors such as income, information and the like[20]. Supply-constraints (c^s) depend on the availability-accessibility of opportunities actually offered by urban planing, which are given at a certain point in time:

$$b = f (p , c^d , c^s)$$

If we adopt *real world choices among various alternatives* as representatives of interest-satisfaction we try to infer the latter from behaviour. The validity of such a strategy depends upon whether constraints are taken into account (are controlled). 'Changers' of behaviour usually provide more meaningful clues than 'constants'. Among the former, those forced by circumstances to change ('forced changers'), among the latter, those willing to make a choice but constrained from action ('frustrated changers'), are of special importance. If an explanation of a certain type of real world choices is available, these strategically important groups are revealed through deviant case analysis. Real world choices related to urban development cover changes of jobs, housing, leisure time, urban and environmental amenities and means of transportation. Migration behaviour seems to be specially suited as a source of information because it usually combines several choices.

Monetary payments for services and goods may be considered as a special form of choice dependent on whether services and goods are for sale. That excludes a large part of the public sector. This implies supply-constraints. Income, on the other hand, is a demand-constraint of paramount importance. Necessary data is provided by household surveys of income and expenditures[21].

Opinions expressed seem the most straightforward approach to interests or preferences. It surely is plausible to ask people whether and why they are happy or unhappy with a given situation and what they wish. Opinions alone, however, will not do. We always have to check opinions expressed against both types of constraints and against relevant behaviour. In order not to violate the rules of 'the art of asking why' a survey has to meet three major requirements:

1. sampling, including not only the target group to be questioned but also relevant control groups
2. emphasis on data analysis[22] beyond pure description (though simple opinion polls remain meaningful when used for explorations)
3. test of hypotheses against actual behaviour through prediction and follow-up studies.

It is a common assertion that people do not know what they want. Naive approaches tend to confirm this. The situation is different if one adopts a strategy such as 'collaborative planning'. It „is similar to the collaborative marketing approach which assumes that the consumer is not sure of his exact desires but would be interested in defining them with the help of a skilled counselor who knows the range of possible alternatives. This brings constraints into play. Nelson N. Foote has contrasted this more advanced marketing approach with the early 'persuasive' or hard sell approach, and the more recent 'listening' or poll taking approach. The parallels with planning are obvious" [23].

Collaborative planning is not just a way of collecting data. It involves planner-client interaction and therefore qualifies as a social planning device.

Survey research often yields concepts of interest closely connected to or represented by background variables such as social status and position in the life-cycle. This way of extracting social indicators has been challenged by empirical findings supporting the view that interests rather should be linked to or expressed by values[24]. Others, however, have demonstrated empirically the importance of socioeconomic status as an indicator of values[25]. In the light of this evidence research should cover both areas.

Allocation of time is another entry into interest-satisfaction, another form of choice. The data basis is provided by time-budget research.

Interest-satisfaction may be approached rather directly through asking respondents to rate their attitude toward each activity. 'Satisfaction' or 'dissatisfaction' then can be assumed to equal the preference rating times the minutes spent in the activity[26]. But once again we have to control for constraints. To achieve such a control it seems useful to split up activities into two groups: obligatory and discretionary activities. The former include, for example, income-related and subsistence activities, the latter comprise recreation, relaxation, socialization etc. The amount of time and the variety reflected in discretionary time allocation may then be interpreted as measures of the quality of life, of course, broken down by social status, sex-work status, and position in the life-cycle (thus accounting for demand-constraints). Supply-constraints can be approached by investigating changes in time-allocation resulting from changes in, say, accessibility. Distance-sensitivity has already been explored, but 'elasticity-analysis' can be extended to other forms of constraints, too.

An interesting experimental technique used is game choice which involves asking respondents „to simulate their choices under certain hypothetical circumstances" (Chapin and Logan). Game data, once again, should be broken down by social groups[27]. This brings as to *gaming results* as social indicators. We already have a variety of environmental gaming simulations at our disposal[28]. They come close to a laboratory setting similar to those available to physical and natural scientists. Gaming simulation allows for the interplay between preferences and constraints. However, before gaming results can be used as social indicators, hypothetical behaviour produced by playing sophisticated 'monopolies' has to be checked against real world or field behaviour. Not only planning students, planning officials, and local legislators should participate in this kind of games but various client groups, too: those for whom the planning is finally done. Participating in simulation and gaming can mean learning for client groups. Although learning research has mainly focussed on management training or work with school children, a tentative link with adults learning has been established[29].

The approaches to interest-satisfaction sketched above are not so much pure strategies. They rather should be applied in combination. Besides, it has always been unwise to put all one's eggs in one methodological basket.

As to the parallels between distributional efficiency and social indicators, both ask for a theoretical basis. We must proceed from verbal to mathematical formulations which are testable[30]. Both lines of assessment must take into account dynamics and social breakdowns of costs and benefits. It seems hard enough to get at the nitty-gritty of basic well-being, but on top of that we also need to know how well-being is changing over time. This is another way of saying that we need to measure social change. „... 'Trend studies' will be a suitable synonym for 'measurement of social change' ... Broadly speaking, he who would measure change has three options. He may refer to existing sources on the variables of interest, he may make new observations, or he may rely on a combination of the two procedures ('replication of baseline studies')"[31]. We agree with Duncan on the last option (which unfortunately is not very popular among researchers) as deserving priority, which of course does not imply a refusal of alternative ways of measuring change. Dealing with dynamics of social costs and benefits involves dealing with prediction. Precision in predicting future costs and benefits is already jeopardized by the very nature of the subject matter, uncertainty, although we have to distinguish varying degrees of predictability: ranging from a definite prediction for specific data to improbabilities and completely unanticipated events[32]. But precision may not even be the most important criterion to judge the quality of predictions as compared to their social function[33]. Forecasts may point to a future problem which will emerge: if things go on like they used to. The forecast itself may trigger off action (by the population or by political decision-makers) which may either support (selffulfilling prophecy) or counteract (self-destroying prophecy) the predicted course of events, for if men define situations as real, they may become real under certain circumstances. We shall be able to study this mechanism at a large scale given the prediction implied in „the Report for the Club of Rome Project."

Social indicators also have a distributional side. Evidence gathered from a goal survey held for the Los Angeles Master Plan[34] can serve to illustrate this. The richer population at large emphasized social costs such as air pollution ('get rid of smog') more than twice as strongly as the poorer negro population. Among the negro population provision of low-cost housing and development of more employment areas ranked twice as high as among the population at large. Research into values conducted by Rokeach and Parker has indicated that differences between negroes and white are primarily related to differences in socio-economic status. If we combine these findings with the opinions expressed, serious doubts arise as to whether programmes to reduce air pollution (and similar social costs) at the expense of economic growth (development of job opportunities and housing production) can win the support of disadvantaged groups such as the negro population. With economic aspirations and expectations rising among negroes, any substantial intervention against economic achievements tends to provoke frustration, aggression and even rebellion[35]. This distributional dilemma of social cost reduction or externality management may be more pronounced in the highly segregated US society but it is by no means unique. It also exists in other societies of the highly industrialized Western European type.

Thus it is only a short way from measurement to policy problems of social indicators.

6. Policy Problems

Better information about social costs and benefits of urban development alone will not do the job — but we badly need it. New technologies can play a vital role in solving or reducing the dilemma described above. Think for example of recycling. But the implementation of any viable program for urban development finally „must be joined to effective political power" and „political commitment to a policy must be sustained" (Friedmann). In the light of this fact planners' role has to be redefined. According to the classical model and conventional planning education, planners restrict their expertise to the elaboration of alternative solutions while leaving both the decision and the implementation to the politicians. Today a new model is emerging according to which planners assume the role of an actor (or agent of social change) during the entire process of political decision-making including plan implementation, while he is engaged in a collaborative relationship to his clients, trying to secure community participation and, if necessary, acting as his clients' advocate[36]

„In action-planning ... the planner moves to the foreground as a person and autonomous agent. His success will in large depend on his skill in managing interpersonal relations" [37]. Besides from that, experiences with advocacy planning have taught us that „the less status, power, and resources held by the client, the more the client is in need of organizing political skills rather than planning skills..." [38].

One would expect studies about community power structures to provide useful know how. But for a decade or two students of (mainly American) communities have been engaged in a controversy about whether local power structures are either oligarchic (with a small group of decision-makers controlling all important issues) or pluralistic (varying elites with varying constituencies controlling varying decisions)[39]. Preoccupation with the power elite controversy has produced only poor practical know how, mainly a short cut to the prediction of decision outcome, treating the decision-making process as a black box, which has nevertheless been applied successfully in a number of cases[40]. Recently Bolan[41] has thrown some light on the black box by formulating hypotheses relating process roles, decision field characteristics, planning and action strategies, and finally, issue attributes, to decision outcome. These hypotheses, informing about constellations tending toward action as against constellations tending toward inaction, have been placed in the context of process steps. Bolan not only summarizes the state of knowledge in the field. He also develops guidelines for future research. Besides Bolan's attempts at generalization we also have evidence from case studies at hand illustrating the social setting in which known generalizations are 'working' and from which new hypotheses are evolving. This has been successfully demonstrated in the case of Coventry by Friend and Jessop[42].

There is evidence that know how for the planning of change is growing across the boundaries of traditional scientific reservations[43]. There are already some universities which offer degree programs in socio-technical system studies[44]. Behavioural foundations of socio-technical systems stem from four bodies of theory and research: system theory, small group theory, job and work system design, influence and 'action-taking' theory.

So if planners engage in incorporating social costs and benefits in urban development planning, they are busy finding out how things really are through trying to change them. They better should see to it, that they are well equiped with new social technologies.

References and Remarks

1) Compare J. Friedmann, A General Theory of Polarized Development, mimeographed paper, School of Architecture and Urban Planning, University of California, Los Angeles 1969: 47 pages; and by the same author, Toward a National Urbanization Policy: Problems, Decisions, and Consequences, Working paper presented at the United Nations Seminar on Financing of Housing and Urban Development, May 25 – June 10 (1970) Copenhagen, 72 pages

2) See again J. Friedmann, The Implementation of Urban-Regional Development Policies: Lessons of Experience, School of Architecture and Urban Planning, University of California, Los Angeles (1971)

3) This distinction has been proposed by H. S. Perloff, „A Framework for Dealing with the Urban Environment: Introductory Statement", in the same (ed.), The Quality of the Urban Environment, Baltimore (1969) p. 3-25

4) M. Echenique, Urban Systems: Toward an Explorative Model, Centre for Environmental Studies, University Working Paper 2 (1969)

5) I. S. Lowry, A Model of Metropolis, Santa Monica (1964)

6) This development has been reviewed in two papers, namely W. Goldner, „The Lowry Model Heritage", Journal of the American Institue of Planners 37 (1971) p. 100-10; and M. Batty, „Recent Developments in Land-Use Modelling: A Review of British Research", Urban Studies (1972) p. 151-77. Recent developments are also reported for other countries, among which Switzerland and the Federal Republic of Germany.

7) Compare among others M. Batty, „Modelling Cities as Dynamic System Nature 231 (1971) p. 425-8 and J. Forrester, Urban Dynamics, Cambridge, Mass. (1969)

8) A. G. Wilson et al., „New Directions in Strategic Transportation Planning", in OECD (ed.), The Urban Transportation Planning Process, Paris (1971) p. 340-1

9) Op. cit. p. 242-3

10) R. U. Ayres and A. V. Kneese, „Pollution and Environmental Quality", in Perloff (ed.), op. cit. p. 35-71

11) U.S. Department of Health, Education, and Welfare, Toward a Social Report, Washington D.C. (1969). See also number 15 of The Public Interest (1969) p. 72-105

12) H. S. Perloff, „New Directions in Social Planning", Journal of the American Institute of Planners 31 (1965) p. 297-304.

13) D. L. Meadows et al., The Limits to Growth. A Report for the Club of Rome Project on the Predicament of Mankind, New York (1972)

14) OECD, Social Indicators Development Programme (Note by the Secretariat), Paris (1971) 12 pages

15) including e.g. demographic concerns

16) D. J. Plessas and R. Fein, „An Evaluation of Social Indicators", Journal of the American Institute of Planners 38 (1972), 43.

17) B. M. Gross, „The State of the Nation: Social Systems Accounting", in R. A. Bauer (ed.), Social Indicators, Cambridge, Mass. and London (1967) p. 220. See also by the same author, The Managing of Organizations, New York (1964)

18) D. E. Boyce, „Toward a Framework for Defining and Applying Urban Indicators in Plan-Making", The Urban Affairs Quarterly (1970) p. 153

19) See J. B. Lansing and R. W. Marans, „Evaluation of Neighborhood Quality", Journal of the American Institute of Planners 35 (1969) p. 195-9

20) Distributional planning is closely linked with the fact that actors' reaction potential with regard to their interest and environment is unequally distributed among socioeconomic groups and varies with position in the life-cycle.

21) The Netherlands have a long tradition of this kind of surveys. Compare Centraal Bureau voor de Statistiek, Nationaal Budgetonderzoek 1963/65, The Hague (1967). For the Common Market see Bureau voor de Statistiek der Europese Gemeenschappen, Budget-Onderzoek 1963/64, Luxemburg (1967)

22) While the tool box for data analysis including theory construction has been considerably expanded in the social sciences, practical applications to survey data rather tend to lag behind. Development of the tool box may be judged from compilations such as R. Boudon, L'Analyse Mathematique des Faits Sociaux, Paris (1967); H. M. Blalock Jr., Theory Construction. From Verbal to Mathematical Formulations, Englewood Cliffs, N.J. (1969); See also the author and H. M. Rodgers, Onderzoek naar Vooruitberekeningsmodellen voor de Interregionale Migratie in Nederland, Netherlands Economic Institute, Rotterdam (1972)

208

23) See D. R. Godschalk and W. E. Mills, ,,A Collaborative Approach to Planning through Urban Activities", Journal of the American Institute of Planners 32 (1966) p. 86. See also N. N. Foote, et al., Housing Choices and Housing Constraints, New York (1960)

24) Compare W. Michelson, ,,An Empirical Analysis of Urban Environmental Preferences", Journal of the American Institute of Planners 32 (1966) p. 355-60; Zvi Maimon, ,,The Inner-City Impact", The Urban Affairs Quarterly (1970): 233-48. There are promising new avenues opened up by the ,,Third Force" group of writers in psychology and psychiatry, alternatives to the Freudian and the experimental-positivistic-behaviouristic approach, see e.g. A.H. Maslow, Toward a Psychology of Being, 2nd ed., New York (1968). The relevance of this alternative approach to planning has been established by R. Stagner, ,,Perceptions, Aspirations, Frustrations, and Satisfactions: An Approach to Urban Indicators", Ekistics 30 (1970) p. 197-9 and W. W. Haythorn, ,,A 'Needs' by 'Sources of Satisfaction' Analysis of Environmental Habitability", Ekistics 30 (1970) p. 200-2. Of course, we must require these alternatives to be made operational and to be tested as explanations of human behavior.

25) See M. Rokeach and S. Parker, ,,Values as Social Indicators of Poverty and Race Relations in America", Ekistics 30 (1970) p. 207-12

26) P. Kranz, ,,What do People do all Day? ", Ekistics 30 (1970) p. 203-6

27) See among others F. S. Chapin Jr., ,,Free Time Activities and Quality of Urban Life", Journal of the American Institute of Planners 37 (1971) p. 411-7; the same author and H. C. Hightower, Household Activity Systems – A Pilot Investigation, Chapel Hill (1966)

28) P. House and P. D. Patterson Jr., ,,An Environmental Gaming-Simulation Laboratory", Journal of the American Institute of Planners 35 (1969) p. 383-8

29) J. Rogers, Adults Learning, Harmondsworth (1971)

30) Compare Blalock, op. cit. For a review of the state-of-the art pertaining to urban-regional development (policy) see the author, ,,Regional Sociology and Regional Planning, Paris and The Hague (Publication and Regional Planning, Paris and The Hague (Publication in collaboration with the United Nations Research Institute for Social Development prepared for 1972)

31) O. D. Duncan, Toward Social Reporting: Next Steps, New York (1969) p. 10

32) With varying degrees of predictability one can also think of varying research provisions to cope with future events. See A. D. Bidermann, ,,Anticipatory Studies and Stand-by Research Capabilities", in Bauer (ed.), op. cit. p. 272-301

33) O. D. Duncan, ,,Social Forecasting – The State of the Art", The Public Interest 17 (1969) p. 88-118

34) Summary Report of the Los Angeles Goals Council, Los Angeles (1969)

35) Stagner, op. cit.

36) The emergence of this new role definition can best be followed by studying the Journal of the American Institute of Planners during the past five years or so.

37) J. Friedmann, „Notes on Societal Action", Journal of the American Institute of Planners 35 (1969) p. 311-8

38) R. S. Bolan, „The Social Relations of the Planner", Journal of the American Institute of Planners 37 (1971) p. 395

39) This substantive controversy has been intertwined with a debate about the best methodological way of identifying local power holders. Compare the author, „Techniken zur Identifizierung lokaler Eliten", Kölner Zeitschrift für Soziologie und Sozialpsychologie 19 (1967), p. 721-35

40) R. C. Hanson, „Predicting a Community Decision: A test of the Miller-Form Theory", American Sociological Review 24 (1959) p. 662-71

41) R. S. Bolan, „Community Decision Behavior: The Culture of Planning" ,Journal of the American Institute of Planners 35 (1969) p. 301-10

42) J. K. Friend and W. N. Jessop, Local Government and Strategic Choice, London (1971)

43) Compare W. G. Bennis et al. (eds.), The Planning of Change, 2nd ed., New York (1969)

44) See for example Graduate School of Business Administration, University of California, Los Angeles, Degree Programs in Socio-Technical System Studies, (1970) 45 pages.

Practical Concepts and Instruments for Social
Committment in Technology Assessment
Directed to Quality of Urban Life

BIG REGIONS OR BIG CITIES

Anders G. Ejerhed
Research Division of the Swedish Association of Engineers and Architects
Stockholm, Sweden

The Swedish Association of Engineers and Architects is engaged in a number of activities in which it is attempting in various ways to contribute to the discussion about the structure of a better society and the means to be used to achieve it. One such discussion is entitled ,,Big Regions or Big Cities? " and the present paper is a brief summary of the ideas which we are trying in various ways to bring out for public discussion.

We have chosen to discuss a concrete example regarding the *Stockholm region*. However, the ideas are applicable to most big cities. We have succeeded in gaining a fairly considerable response for this alternative method of solving the problems of the big city.

I would like to give two introductory comments. This is not going to be a technically advanced report, only describing means of transportation. The advanced passenger trains (APT) is the key element in our alternative but still it is only one element in a big system. Secondly, do not expect a technology assessment of APT with quantified factors etc because this has not yet been done, it belongs to the debate going on in Sweden.

Many people fear that the big cities of the future will be chaotic urban jungles, in which the side effects of urbanization will get out of control and vital functions will come to a standstill. The consequences of urban growth can be described as in Fig. 1.

The following is a specific Stockholm example of the side effects of urban growth. The linking of two motorways at an interchange junction will require an area of 1 km² located only 4 to 5 km from the city centre. The

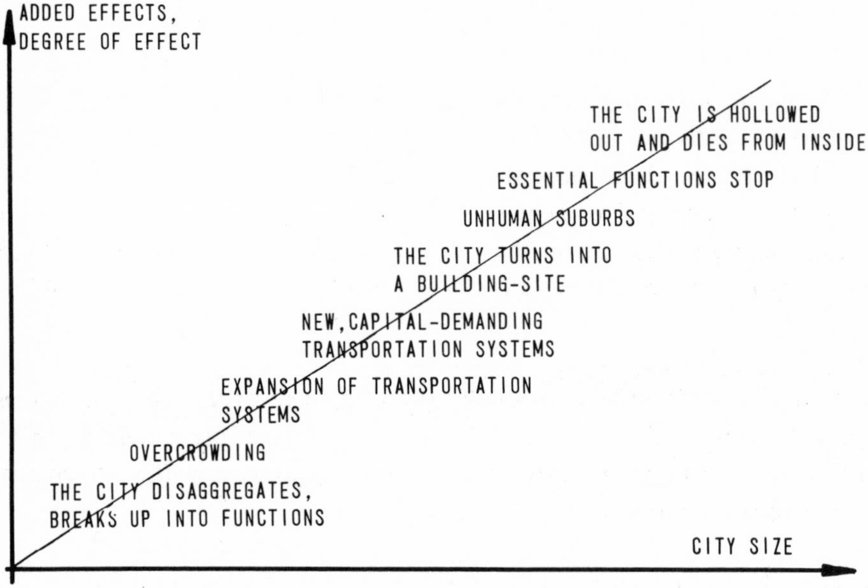

Fig 1: Consequences of urban growth

remedy against such monstrous constructions is to not build big cities. Towns of a reasonable size avoid these problems, simply because their inhabitants do not need to travel so much.

The problem with urban growth can be summarized as follows. With increasing urban population the price of centrally located building ground will go up. Those living in the centre of an urban area are forced away due to unproportionally high dwelling costs and business and administration move in. Large investments in transportation are needed to enable people to get in touch with different functions in society. To pay off these huge investments in infra-structure more houses have to be built concentrically from the city centre which means more and more transportation and so on.

The alternative is to link together towns of moderate size to form an urban zone, i.e. an area in which people can meet within a reasonable time, for example, within an hour. People evidently are more time-sensitive than distance-sensitive; studies of how the individual decides on his 'transport pattern' support this theory. In an urban zone the essential functions of the capital city can be conveniently used, even if one lives and works somewhere else in the zone. This combines the advantages of the big city and the small town, while avoiding the disadvantages. We now have the opportunity to do this. New technology allows for the use of advanced passenger trains (APT-trains), which substantially reduce the travelling time. The carriage of an APT-train is tilted 9-12° in relation to the boggies when the train goes through curves. Together with a slightly altered boggie construction this enables the train to go 220 km per hour.

Stockholm is situated at the mouth of a large lake (Mälaren), which runs far inland. Around it, there are also a number of smaller towns (see Fig. 2 a). According to suggested regional plans Stockholm shall expand in the next 10-15 years according to either of two similar alternatives (see Fig. 2b,c). With fast trains connecting the towns around the Mälar, and perhaps a few other ones too, the assumed expansion of Stockholm can take place in the whole Mälar Valley.

The main advantage of the new transportation technology to be implemented – the APT-trains – would be the favourable conditions one gets for the building of a future society (see Fig. 2d). The advantage of the

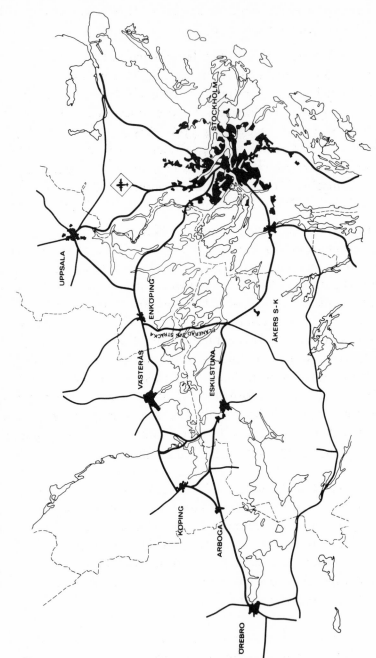

Fig. 2 a: Stockholm and the lake Mälar Valley, year 1970

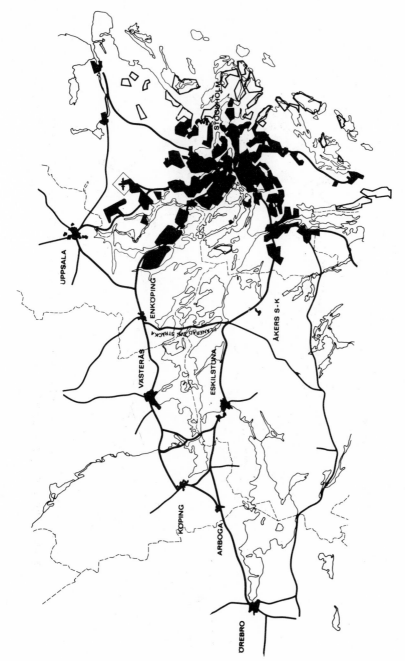

Fig 2 b: Distribution of population, year 2000, a suggestion for a regional plan, alternative ,,spread out"

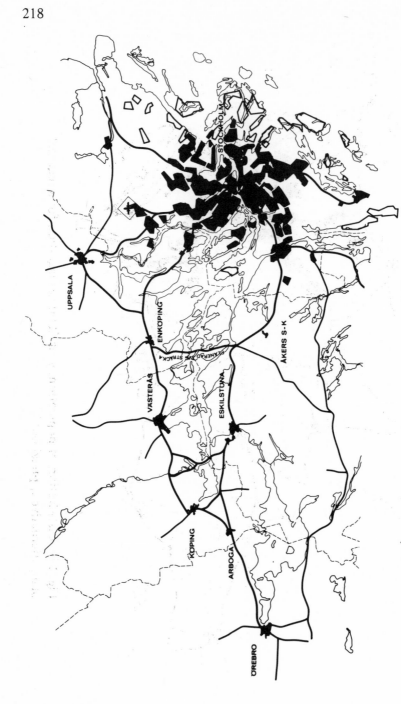

Fig 2 c: Distribution of population, year 2000, a suggestion for a regional plan, alternative „compact"

219

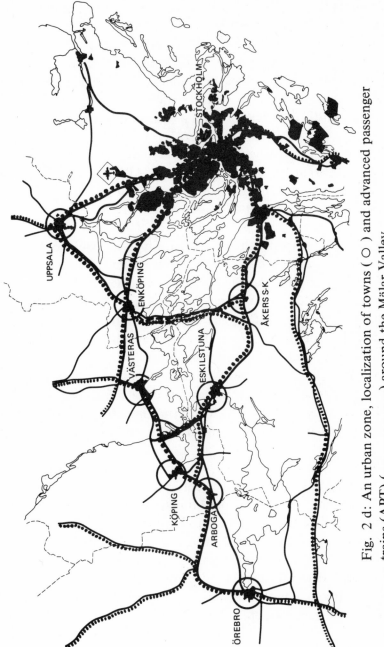

Fig. 2 d: An urban zone, localization of towns (O) and advanced passenger trains (APT) (································) around the Mälar Valley

train itself is mainly reduced travelling time. APT-trains will allow for the expansion of the Stockholm conurbation to include the entire Mälaren valley Enköping, Västeroas, Eskilstuna, Uppsala and Stockholm will be so close to each other that it will be quite realistic to deal with them as a single urban region, sharing many service installations and having a richly diversified labour market in common. The Mälaren valley will be the common city park and on the peripheries of these towns there will be large, undisturbed areas of natural scenery of various types.

But do not greater distances result in more frequent and longer journeys? This may seem to be the case. But the APT-trains will make it possible to plan so as to avoid long journeys as much as possible; we may live in a central position in relation to our own interests.

As a rule the towns should be self-supplying with jobs. People of more specialized professions will have to count on increased travelling in distance, but not in time. Each town will be able to offer culture amenities within its own circle, recreation facilities, shopping centres a.s.o. But to consume professional culture of international class or to buy in specialized shops one would have to leave the local area. Everyone will be able to reach all parts of the region within a relatively short time (see Fig. 3). The feeling of nearness, of having facilities within reach at a moderate cost, is perhaps more important than we think. The urbanization of the Mälaren valley may have a decentralizing effect in terms of space but it will nevertheless involve a centralization of functions.

Modern technology is developing in a technical environment and is producing advanced management systems for technology itself but also for economy, politics or social functions. The growth of the capital city is primarily determined by the growth of these administrative systems. The technical production units, on the other hand, have to move out for lack of space. The only enterprises to stay in the big city will be those which require a richly differentiated labour market and need little land, which make only moderate demands on the environment, which have a limited volume of transport, etc.

Who is to pay for the APT-trains? Naturally, those who benefit from them. Those who are spared the need to rebuild the central parts of the

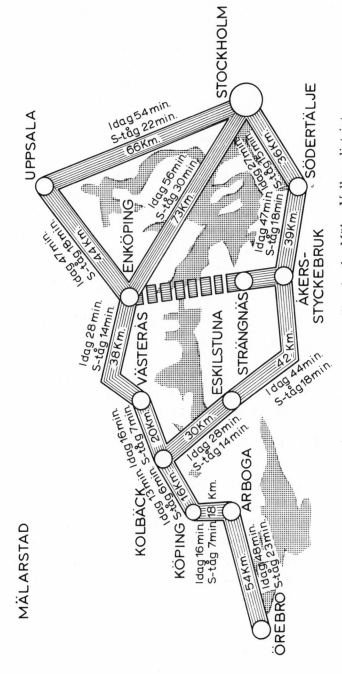

Fig. 3: Distances and time for travelling in the Mälar Valley district
Idag=today, S-tåg = APT – trains (160 km/h)

big cities to provide for twice the volume of traffic. Those who avoid having traffic-weary colleagues at work, those who benefit from the greater facilities and the richer life of the small town, those who own ground close to where APT-trains run and thus get an unearned increment, and, finally, those who travel on the trains.

APT-trains covering all of Sweden would cost quite a lot, but regarded in a wider context, a reduction of not more than 0,5% of the costs of road traffic in the year 1980 would cover both the interest and the mortage. The external benefits of a network of APT-trains would be considerable and probably of the same magnitude as the costs. It is politically and psychologically easier to accept the idea of APT-trains if one divides the costs on those who get the external benefits and the passengers. In the 1890's this philosophy of railroad economy was used all over the world including in Sweden and led to sound decisions and investments. Gradually rail-road ventures have been looked upon more and more as isolated companies or profit centres. One has forgotten that means of transportation is part of a system — the society — and this part has to be linked to the system in an economically logical way.

But why APT-trains and not trains based on a more advanced technology like air cushions? The Stockholm region has old rail-roads in rather a good condition. By putting new trains on these rails new life is given to old investments, already paid off a long time ago. Thus APT-trains can be run quite cheaply (cf. Appendix).

There is reason to believe that these new conditions for town planning may yield great financial gains. The big city is said to be productive. True, but the yearly increase in total productivity must in the city to a large extent be used to rebuild and re-rebuild the city. Consequently the room for increase in private consumption becomes smaller and smaller for each city inhabitant as the city grows. The urban zone is something in between city and country, an alternative that combines high productivity with big room for increases in private consumption.

It is probably quite futile to try to stop the urbanization of the Stockholm region by directives. An alternative that is more attractive than today's big, growing city has to be created.

There is much evidence that in an expanded urban zone of the kind I have described we shall have substantially greater possibilities to satisfy the demand for good contacts *as well as* detachment. The successor of the city is the urban zone which has been welded by modern technology into *a unit* — and we have every reason to assume that it is the only correct environment for modern man. Here he will be set free from his local dependence and will be able to attain the freedom which all the possibilities of choice in the urban zone provide. These possibilities include free and unpolluted countryside, which is difficult to reach for the inhabitant of a big-city.

The big problem of putting the idea of 'Mälaren City' into existence is that there is today nobody — either on the political, administrative or economic side — who has the authority or is competent to take up the question of joint-planning. That is what we are trying to initiate and we are progressing favourably.

Summary

1. One probably can not have a good Quality of Life rating as an urban inhabitant in too large a city. No community has so far managed to direct modern urbanization along lines that people think give them a good environment. Urbanization in the form of zones might open up new possibilities, this has to be explored. Transport technology is one essential condition for such an alternative urbanization.

2. Society has to view means of transport as a part of a system, not as an isolated 'profit centre'. If the assessment of transport technology isn't based on a system concept it will be uninteresting and falsely directed.

3. Society lacks bodies who interest themselves in finding alternatives, making technology assessment and — provided the alternative has values superior to the way we solve the problems today — who can in the region turn the alternative into reality.

Appendix

AN URBAN ZONE – ESTIMATE OF COSTS FOR APT-TRAINS

Basic assumptions

Seven towns around the Mälar valley are today linked together by a seldom used railway. New investments in rails and trains for this railway-route are assumed to be done in several stages. The figures in the following calculation reflect a powerful urban-zone venture, i.e. we assume a timetable with frequent travelling facilities on very comfortable trains, together with a rapid increase in travelling speed. Those assumptions, which one can add up to a *service-policy,* are realistic only in combination with a different *financing-fare policy,* i.e. when costs are carried not only by passengers but also by those who get the external benefits (landowners, companies, communities etc).

All costs are calculated high and can probably be reduced somewhat, e.g. with lighter and simpler carriages combined with a capacity more adapted to the needs expenditures can be decreased.

If one choses to start the implementation of APT-trains on a shorter distance (e.g. Stockholm-Enköping 73 km) one can go to stage '200 km/h' immediately. Investment cost in rails are low because of the limited distance, the technique for APT-trains is already developed and trains can be running 2-4 years after the decision. This first railway-line would, with a proper service and fare policy, quickly generate a demand for extension to other towns. Thus the stages might as well be in terms of network length (given the speed) and not speed (given the network).

Stage 'O'

An example of the changes in *service* that can be done today, with the existing *financing-fare*-policy, is one additional train at night-time on part of the route (Stockholm-Eskilstuna) together with a slight modernization of the signal-system to make the operation of it less personel-intensive and thus cut over-time wages. Such a project would probabbly balance around the break-even point.

Stage '130 km/h', approximately 2 years from now

Out of 275 km of *rail* connecting the seven towns, 80 km have to be replaced to facilitate speeds of 130 km/h. A number of new trains *(APT trains)* with high comfort, technically capable of a speed up to 160 km/h, capacity for 150 passengers will be needed. No changes in *signal system.*

The facility offered is one train in each direction (south and north) leaving Stockholm every hour from 6 a.m. − 10 p.m. for a roundtrip which takes 2 hrs 40 min (Stockholm-Eskilstuna 60 min, Stockholm-Västeraos 58 min).

Investments amounting to 65 MSwCr will be needed (4 APT-trains, 25 rails) with a yearly capital cost of 6 MSwCr. Operating and maintenance cost is estimated to be roughly 28 MSwCr (for a capacity of 5000 seats per day).

Stage '160 km/h', approximately 7-8 years from now

By exchanging the rail the speed can be increased from 130 to 220 km/h.

The rail on roughly half of the distance must be straightened out, the cost/km is about five times as much as for renewing but it also shortens the distance by approximately 20 km. On the other half of the rail *safety measures* (changing level crossing and signal system) must be taken.

The same running frequency is offered, a roundtrip takes 2 hrs and 10 min. (Stockholm-Västeraos 49 min.)

Investments will be 185 MSwCr (165 new rail, 20 safety) with a capital cost of 17 MSwCr. Operating and maintenance cost approximately 32 MSwCr (for a capacity of 5000 seats per day).

Stage '220 km/h', 10-15 years from now

New *APT-trains,* equal to those capable of 160 km/h but with a maximum speed of 220 km/h, will be needed.

Running frequency is one train in each direction per hour. A roundtrip takes 1 hr and 30 min, (Stockholm-Eskilstuna 38 min, Stockholm-Västeraos 37 min).

Investments are in new trains, 55 MSwCr, giving a capital cost of 6 MSwCr per year. Operating and maintenance is somewhat cheaper per passenger seat/km due to the higher speed, approximately 28 MSwCr.

Summary (all figures are approximate but have the correct order of magnitude)

(MSwCr)	Stage	130	160	220
Rails etc		2	16	16
Trains		4	4	6
Operating and maintenance		25-30	30-35	25-30
Total (yearly cost)		30-35	50-55	approx.50
Cost (SwCr) per passenger seat km		approx.0,07	approx.0,10	approx.0.09

Comments on financing-fare-policy

Let Enköping be connected to Stockholm with APT-trains going 220 km/h and a running-frequency equal to that previously assumed. Then the use and thus the impact of this facility will be determined very much by the fare-policy.

(Assume total yearly costs of approx 14 MSwCr when offering 7000 seats per day, i.e. 5 SwCr per single trip.)

Return-trips at a realistic 50% utilization would be 20 SwCr if all costs were to be covered by the fare.

If the total expenditures are financed by taxes the inhabitants of Enköping would pay roughly 900 SwCr per person.

If the costs are to be paid by ground increment in the central part of Enköping, say within a circle having a 1 km radius from the very town centre, 4 SwCr per m^2 and year would be sufficient.

A mix of financing to cover total expenditures could be e.g.

60% contribution from ground increment
20% contribution from taxes
20% contribution from tickets.

A person living in Enköping, working in Stockholm would pay 80 SwCr for a one-month-ticket. His taxes would go up 200 SwCr per year and if he occupied an average flat near the town his rent would increase about 3-4%.

These percentage figures do not claim to be a very wellbased assumption but merely indicating one way to distribute costs. It is reasonable to believe that the ground increment will be higher than 4 SwCr/m^2,year. In that case the whole APT-railway project is financed by ground increment.

NEW TRANSPORTATION TECHNIQUES FOR THE EIGHTIES: „TRANSRAPID" AND „TRANSURBAN"

Dieter Haseke
Krauss-Maffei A.G.,
München, Federal Republic of Germany

Interlocal transit — a term suggesting motion and mobility — has been increasingly subject to change during recent years. Due to the rapid progress made so far, especially in the field of technology and theoretical analysis, the realization of plans for systems meeting the future transport requirements will be possible in the near future.

In this connection, the fundamental question arises: Why novel transportation systems?

Statistical forecasts of international institutions are unanimous in that increased leisure time, growing mobility and more and more division of labour within the next few decades give reason to expect an extraordinary increase in the demand for transportation facilities.

At the same time, *the carriers and users expect*

— increased speed, respectively short travel times
— short waiting times (high frequency of operation)
— more riding comfort
— optimal safety.

Desirable features *from the point of view of the operator are:*

— low operating and maintenance costs
— low specific investment costs
— possibility of integration with other transportation systems

- system flexibility through adaptability to changed traffic conditions
- capability of fully automatic operation.

Finally, *from the point of view of environmental protection,* the catalogue of requirements which must be met by an adequate means of transport comprises the following major items:

- no air pollution by exhaust gases
- low noise level inside and outside the system
- no contamination through abraided rubber
- integration into the architecture of cities and preservation of countryside.

Considering these requirements and looking at the present-day traffic situation with its alarming prospects for the time to come, only completely novel transportation systems which are not burdened by outdated notions and are especially designed to cope with future transportation tasks could have the capability of providing the optimum solution to the problem. Transportation systems must rapidly and efficiently link up congested areas and start where the existing and well-proven means of transport are approaching their economic, physical, psychological or capacity limits and will thus provide a meaningful as well as urgent supplement and relief to the present traffic situation.

The German Krauss-Maffei AG has for some years been occupied on a broad basis with the research and development of new transportation systems and concepts.

One of the areas on which Krauss-Maffei has concentrated its efforts is the magnetically levitated unconventional high-speed ground transportation system, called TRANSRAPID, for intercity transport at speeds up to 300 mph.

The second area of concentrated effort is a new urban means of comfortable mass transport called TRANSURBAN.

Both systems are unconventional primarily because they use vehicles supported and guided by electronically controlled electromagnets without any physical contact with the guideway and propelled by linear induction motors without noise and exhaust gases.

With regard to TRANSRAPID, i.e. the system and its stages of technological development, the following can be said:

The operational concept: direct services by relatively small units at high frequencies; to ensure better economic utilization of the infrastructure, both passengers and goods will be caried.

Possible applications are seen as follows:

First and foremost, the system should be used for high-speed intercity transit over distances of between 200 and 1200 km, with the object of making business and duty travel over these distances possible *within a day*. Within these distance limits the magnetic trains will be faster than a modern aircraft.

During hours of low passenger traffic the vehicles would carry urgent containerizable goods, so as to cut specific transport costs by good utilization of the infrastructure throughout the day. The vehicles run on separate main lines, which they leave only at their destination to drive into the city center on their own tracks. All operation is fully automatic and is controlled by central computers.

The second possible application is as a rail link between city centers and the airports that are moving further and further away from them. An airport 60 km distant could be reached safely in approx. 8 to 10 minutes. This is one example that the system is not intended to displace the proven transport modes — motor car, railway, aircraft — but to supplement and overlie them in useful manner and above all to handle the extra demand for high-speed travel that will confront us in the coming decades.

On the question of the cost of the new high-speed tracked systems, all that will be said here is that with their prefabricated elevated tracks without intersections, their no-contact technique — i.e. minimum personnel requirements — magnetic cushion tracked systems present an unexpectedly attractive cost picture. Passenger-mile costs are well below air fares and, assuming a comparable calculation system, will most probably lie somewhere around the First Class rail fares.

Let us now look at the various stages of development which led to the present results.

As early as end of the year 1969, Krauss-Maffei constructed the first model transport system of the world with an electro-magnetic support and guidance system and propelled by a linear induction motor.

Knowledge and experience gained and secured through a great number of experiments at various test stands led to the construction in 1971 of a test plant consisting of a 1000 m test track and the magnetic-cushion vehicle, called TRANSRAPID 02, having a weight of 11 tons and a length of 12 m. It was not later than a few weeks afterwards when, due to the short distance to be covered, the theoretical maximum speed of 164 km per hour could be reached without any change in the magnetic levitation and propulsion system being necessary.

A novel power pick-off system ensures the uninterrupted transmission of electric power even at high speed levels. The vehicle cell is suspended on the chassis frame by means of a secondary suspension system with pneumatic springs and vibration dampers.

The track and vehicle concept permits relatively realistic statements. The test results achieved so far have shown that the requirements to be met by the system have been fully satisfied. Transportation experts, politicians and technicians from all over the world have satisfied themselves about the efficiency of the system.

Tests are not being confined to the electro-magnetic system. Since September 1972 an air-cushion vehicle of the same size as the magnetic-cushion vehicle 02 is being tested on KM's bivalent test plant for the purpose of making a comparison as exactly and objectively as possible between the two contactless magnetic- and air-cushion systems.

By spring 1973 this facility will be supplemented by a new elevated track with a length of 2500 m on which the magnetic vehicle TRANSRAPID 04

Fig 1: Traveling Distances in Europe

will attain a speed in the range of about 350 km per hour. This is considered to be a necessary intermediate step in view of the final test carried out at the central test facility at Donauried where for the first time a standard-size large test vehicle attaining speeds of 500 km per hour is to be put into operation for long run tests in the years 1974 and 1975.

Talking about the development of and the achievements made in connection with the TRANSRAPID system, I would now like to proceed to a short account of how the TRANSURBAN system ·will solve future transportation problems and meet the requirements mentioned before.

Krauss-Maffei has developed three TRANSURBAN variants in order to be able to cover a broad area of transportation requirements. The first variant, the *TRANSURBAN Moving Lane System,* has been designed for comfortable mass transport with extremely high traffic density (capacity: up to 40000 passengers/hour; cruising speed: up to 12 mph).

The second variant, the *TRANSURBAN Non-Stop System,* is a high-speed means of transport to link up two or several areas with a great demand for transportation facilities; for example, downtown areas with major suburban parking areas, shopping or sports centers and satellite towns. The capacity of this system is lower by comparison with the moving lane, but its cruising speed is higher.

The third variant, the *TRANSURBAN Takt System,* serves large metropolitan areas and is able to adjust itself to the traffic density, which decreases from the central to the peripheral parts of the city, while at the same time providing a good passenger carrying capacity and a good load factor at all times.

Let us take a more detailed look at the variant Takt.

Here we have a transportation concept whose principal purpose is to serve large metropolitan areas. In order to serve areas of different traffic density equally well —— both technically and economically —— we started out with the following basic concept:

Passenger transportation is handled by vehicle units providing 6 to 18 seats. Depending on traffic density, these vehicles can be compounded to

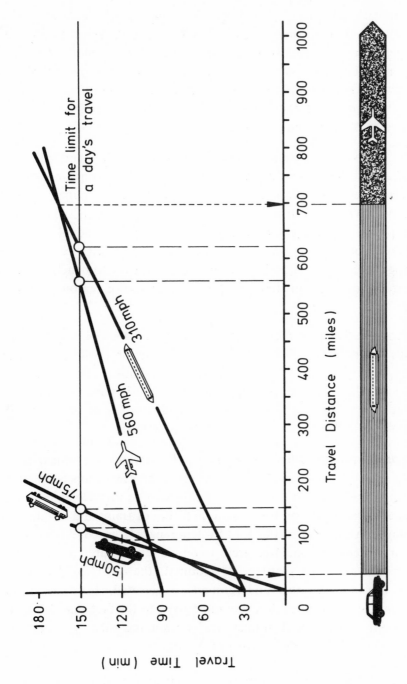

Fig 2: Travel Time with different Modes of Transportation

form more or less long trains or can also operate individually. On their way from the downtown areas, where there is a great demand for transportation, to the peripheral areas of the city, these trains split up into smaller units until only a single vehicle moves into a loop in some far-out suburb where the demand for transportation is correspondingly small. The individual vehicles are gradually rejoined to form a full train as they make their way back to the center of the city.

With this type of transport, which is pre-programmed and cannot be influenced by the passenger, every vehicle is like a 'through coach' on a particular line. The compound trains run at a predetermined cycle (in German: Takt). The shortest interval is around 30 seconds, which means that both the trains in the downtown area and the individual vehicles in the suburbs operate at exactly the same cycle, only with very different capacities. Even in the suburbs, passengers do not have to benefit from the lower traffic densities in these areas at the expense of reasonable waiting times.

The second variant, the *TRANSURBAN Non-Stop System,* is a high-speed intervals during rush hour traffic and at greater intervals, such as two minutes, during periods of less intensive traffic. This is also a meaningful method to adapt the system to demand for transit services which varies with the time of the day. The splitting-up and rejoining of trains as well as the entire operation of the system are fully automatic.

In contrast with the other two variants, the stations are similar to our present subway and commuter train stations. The trains stop at the platform for alighting and boarding. The system is very flexible in terms of capacity. Depending on the maximum length of trains and frequency of operation, the capacity of the Takt System ranges from 18,000 passengers per hour in densely populated areas to only a few hundred passengers per hour in the suburban districts. If required, the TRANSURBAN Takt System can also be run underground or elevated. For underground operation, particular attention should be given to the fact that this system requires only half as much tunnel cross-section as a subway system. This fact has a decisive bearing on investment costs.

However, city planners and carriers are also interested in the economics of such a system. Initial calculations have revealed that the investment,

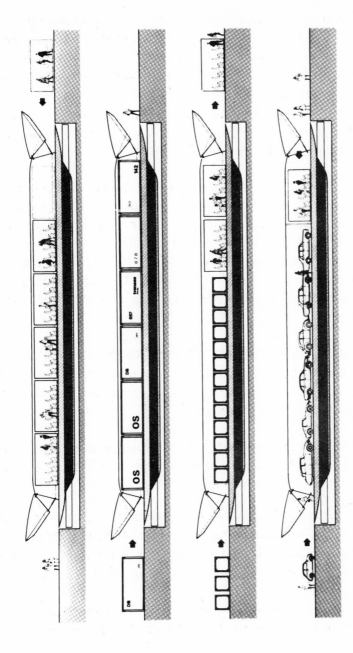

Fig 3: TRANSRAPID – Optimum utilization of system capacity due to multi – purpose application for passenger, freight and mixed traffic

operating and maintenance costs of such systems operated on the basis of the magnetic levitation technique are more favourable than the cost of comparable classical means of transport. These results appear credible if one considers that magnetic levitation through better load distribution requires a much lighter infrastructure, that contact-free operation has a great effect on wear and thus considerably reduces maintenance costs of both guideway and vehicle. Finally, automatic system operation accounts for an extremely low manpower requirement.

An important requirement placed on new means of transport is their compatibility with existing transit systems and environmental conditions. Therefore it is important to make it clear that these systems are not supposed to supersede old and proven transit systems but to complement them in a meaningful manner and to handle the additional traffic volume which we shall be faced with in the decades to come. Initially, they will only be introduced if new demands arise and even then only on a step-by-step basis.

I talked about TRANSRAPID, TRANSURBAN, about unconventional transportation systems in general and — among others — about environmental aspects. Concluding, please allow me to give still some remarks especially concerning the last point.

If you compare conventional and unconventional means of transport relative to their effect on the environment, you will get the following result:

Only automobiles and aircrafts show a noticeable amount of exhaust gas emission, which is non-existent in the case of the magnetically levitated and propelled TRANSRAPID and TRANSURBAN systems. The same applies to fall-out products, such as dust, abraded rubber, etc..

In evaluating the sound level as a factor of disturbance in terms of environmental protection, the railroad must also be included.

Road traffic and the traffic surface area created for this purpose characterize the image of a city to considerable extent; the consequence is a growing decrease in space available for city parks and recreational areas.

Furthermore, the landscape, even though to only a limited extent, is adversely affected by large airports, which in turn is not true of the future unconventional track-bound systems.

A significant improvement of existing systems with respect to environmental protection will only be possible with considerable financial effort and require a considerable amount of time.

If, in addition to the advantage of having very little detrimental effects on the environment, one also considers the aspect of economics, the introduction of new technologies in the field of transport should be pushed ahead with greater speed.

ASSESSING THE IMPACT OF
FUTURE PUBLIC SERVICE SYSTEMS
BY SIMULATION

Robin Roy
Faculty of Technology, The Open University
Bletchley Bucks, United Kingdom

Introduction

This paper reports on some exploratory experiments designed to develop a method for obtaining human responses to new man-machine systems at the pre-design stage. Some preliminary results of tests on a computerized public information system and various new forms of urban transport system are given.

The need for better methods for designing and planning complex systems of people and technology is evident from the examples of past innovations which have either failed to produce the benefits expected, do not meet any real social need, or have given rist to unwanted social, environmental and other side-effects.

It is only necessary to consider the disappointing performance of many of the existing systems using computers to find examples. For instance, many computer-aided instruction systems have turned out to be expensive 'white elephants' because of a failure to predict the type of soft-ware required, and that changes would be needed in the organization of schools and in the training of teachers[1].

Existing types of computer-aided design system, looked at by Cooley[2] from a trade unionist's viewpoint, far from offering the benefits of reduced drudgery, increased work satisfaction and more leisure, require their operators to work 24 hour shifts at a high tempo and result in less job satisfaction because of a greater division of labour.

In the field of aircraft technology, supersonic airliners have been built, at enormous cost, not only without prior verified evidence that the environmental effects would be acceptable or that passengers want them, but also without adequate consideration of human factors, for example, the physiological effects of supersonic flight or their vulnerability to highjacking.

These failures arise from over — enthusiastic development, (coupled with over-selling), of new technologies as soon as they seemed feasible, for reasons of adventure, profit or both without paying enough attention to the human part of the resulting systems — both the needs of the individual user and the impact on society. As a result we find vast sums spent on developing systems which in practice do not 'work' satisfactorily when exposed to the complexity of real world human needs and behaviour. By then of course it is usually too late and people either have to learn to live with and adapt to the new system or it becomes an expensive mistake that no-one wants.

Can we avoid making more mistakes of this kind in the future? Technologies currently under development mean that very many new systems can be expected to burst upon society over the next decades. For example, Gordon and Helmer's[3] now famous Delphi study predicted that in industrialized nations the following developments in automation were likely to occur before the end of the century:

- direct links from shops to banks to check credit and record trans-
  actions.
- widespread use of sophisticated teaching machines.
- automation of office work and services leading to displacement of
  25% of current work force.
- automation of libraries looking up and reproducing copy.
- automated rapid transit.
- automatic interpretation of medical symptoms.
- automated voting in the sense of legislating through automated
  plebiscite.

The benefits of introducing such systems are as yet unproven, while the needs of their potential users and their possible side-effects are as yet unknown. Perhaps the new technology permitting the development of the above systems should be used to create totally different kinds of banking, educational, information and medical services. If so we should like to know what form these services could and should take.

Pre-Testing Methods

Given the desirability of obtaining the responses of those affected to new systems before attempting to develop them, what methods are available?

Surveys and polls of the opinions of people who had not had experience of a new system are notoriously unreliable. One need only recall the insurmountable obstacles predicted for the acceptance of the horseless carriage, television and the telephone. In order to obtain realistic responses some way of providing those affected with experience of the system is necessary.

An obvious approach is to build and test a prototype system. A good example of this approach is Project Intrex[6] at the Massachusetts Institute of Technology, under which a prototype remote-access library has been set up and is being developed using feedback from realworld trials.

Others have suggested that the only reliable way of testing new technologies is through large-scale social experimentation in which volunteers would live in Experimental[7] or Test Cities[8] containing a variety of prototype systems and services. Such communities would allow people to experience, evaluate and *reject* if necessary, the new ways of living offered by such innovations as computer networks, closed-circuit waste recycling, movable housing and so on.

The above approaches raise three major problems. First, how do we design and build prototype systems without prior feedback on the type of system required by users? Second, once built, our prototypes can only be modified with difficulty. Third, it is of course only possible to build to the limit of currently available technology, whilst we may be interested in the possibilities offered by some future technology.

These difficulties have been overcome in other fields through the simple expedient of simulation. Comparatively simple and cheap simulations[9] can often be devised which will provide the information necessary to guide the development of real systems.

The remainder of this paper describes a project conducted at the Design Research Laboratory[10], UMIST, to develop a simulation technique suitable for examining the behaviour of possible future man-machine systems.

The Project

The project itself was concerned with evaluating two kinds of systems which are currently being developed — a computerized public information service and various new urban transport systems — from the point of view of their potential users. In particular we were interested in basic performance requirements, user preferences and characteristic modes of system behaviour. We required therefore to find out how and why people might interact with the system and what their reactions and difficulties might be. All that was required was a simulation of those hardware and software features of a prototype system that a person would perceive when using it, plus life situations in which a need to use the system arose.

It is important to note that we sought gross patterns of user behaviour with which any real system would have to cope. These patterns are dependent on the total characteristics of the man-machine system, (in particular the characteristics of the people in the system), rather than on the details of the hardware. Thus the hardware of the system need only be simulated roughly at first. The highly variable part of the real system — the human component — was included in the simulation in the form of human participants.

Simulation of a computerized public information service

The first experiments examined the behaviour of various possible types of service which would give the public access via remote terminals to a range of computer-stored information.

The method of simulation was derived from earlier work on pre-testing computer-aided design systems[11], in which the 'computer' was simulated by a team of human experts and the 'terminal' was a closed-circuit television screen plus intercom, via which written and verbal messages could be exchanged between user and 'computer'.

By varying the rules of operation a variety of existing and hypothetical systems could be simulated. For example, in the experiments three modes of interaction were tested. These were input and output using visual material, (simulating a teletype plus video display); voice input, visual output, (simulating a hypothetical voice translation device plus video display); and voice input and output (simulating a hypothetical voice translation and answer-back device).

Prior to the trials the test users, who were final year school students, had selected problems, (which involved obtaining information or advice), that they actually wished to resolve. These included finding a summer job; making a tax enquiry; and making travel arrangements. They could either obtain the service required by making enquiries from existing facilities or by using the simulated information service. The users kept a record of their actions, difficulties and impressions during both real and simulated trips, and a record of the messages sent between users and 'computer' was also made.

No restrictions were placed on the content or language of messages. This was because in these exploratory experiments we wanted information on the requirements for an idealized no-learning system.

Although the main purpose of the experiments was to develop the simulation method, some interesting results were obtained. Perhaps the most marked was that the users, who were all of above average intelligence, were often unsure both of what questions to ask in order to resolve their particular problem and how to phrase their enquiry clearly. The 'computer' had to compensate by interrogating the users to define their precise need.

Having identified their need it was found that users could obtain a complete and satisfactory answer more surely if the computer prompted them or asked all of the questions. When users asked the questions, the 'computer' often had to intervene to prevent a misleading line of enquiry being followed.

The 'computer's' pedantic responses, (in answering every trivial point), unnerved some users, particularly since there was a delay between question and response. Generally, however, delay times of between half and one minute were reported to be acceptable. Longer delays were particularly annoying if users felt that they were being ignored, and some commented that they should like some immediate indication of how long they would have to wait, so that they could carry on with some other activity.

Users reported that interaction with a 'machine' had a great advantage over their experiences with person to person communication, (either face to face or over the telephone), in that they had time to stop and think between questions without feeling under any social pressure to hurry. This was particularly true for the voice input, written output mode of interaction, which all the users said they preferred.

In a follow-up discussion all the users were enthusiastic about the possibility of a real computerized information system being available, mainly for its advantages of convenience and speed over existing sources. Perhaps not unexpectedly their main reservation concerned the problem of confiding personal information without knowing who might have access to it.

It would appear then, from these experiments, that the proponents of a future public computer 'utility', dispensing information and services via linked terminals, should take into account the difficulties that users are likely to have in diagnosing their particular problems. Apart from when factual and unambiguous information is wanted, users will probably need to have access to highly skilled human problem diagnosticians who would process the enquiry before machine retrieval. Nevertheless, computerized public information systems could potentially offer benefits, not only in terms of convenience, but in making information more accessible, in particular to those who have social or other difficulties in using conventional sources. This latter hypothesis of course requires further investigation.

Simulation of new urban transport systems

The second series of experiments involved developing the basic simulation idea in order to evaluate a number of new urban transport systems in combinations that have been proposed as offering a long-term solution to the problem of traffic in towns. Some of these systems have already reached the prototype vehicle stage without ever having had their basic performance characteristics and acceptability tested.

Four basic types of system were studied:

1. *,personal transit' systems* consisting of small vehicles, available on demand, which run under automatic guidance on a light-weight track. (As represented by the four-seat ,Cabtrack' system in the U.K. and a variety of similar systems in the U.S.A.).

2. *'dual-mode personal transit' systems,* which can be driven manually on ordinary roads or guided automatically on the same track as the single-mode vehicles. (A system similar to this was developed under the name Alden StaRRcar).

3. *Small town cars,* (probably electric powered), which would be available at hire points to accredited drivers.

4. An *on-demand mini-bus system,* similar to a radio taxi service. The bus could be called from home or from special public telephones. (Various 'dial-a-bus' systems are currently undergoing trials in many parts of the world).

Since, as before, we were interested in the gross aspects of system behaviour, the hardware of the transport simulator was kept simple. Essentially it consisted of a sequence of visual displays, (maps and slides), for each type of system, which guided the user step by step *in real-time* through various rooms representing the various stages of a journey. For example, to make a simulated ,Cabtrack' journey from home to work, the user would locate his preferred 'cabstop' on a map in the 'home' room, go from there into the 'access' room, where he would see a series of slides depicting the walking and waiting involved. When a vehicle slide appeared, he would enter the 'vehicle' room and sit down to another set of slides depicting the view from the vehicle until a time display indicated arrival at the destination.

Had the user decided instead of walking, to go by dial-a-bus to the stop he would have gone through a dial-a-bus sequence before the Cabtrack' sequence.

The purpose of the simulator was not to reproduce the actual travelling experience, but to give the user a *feel* for the process of using various systems and for their basic performance characteristics. These characteristics, (e.g. vehicle speed, walking distance), could be varied simply by altering the timing and/or sequence of displays.

We were also interested in the users' choice of travel mode under a variety of life circumstances and in the effect that access to the new facilities might have on the day-to-day activity patterns of users. Would they, for example, travel more or less? Would they want to use private cars sometimes? And so on. Consequently a considerable amount of effort was spent on developing an activity simulation 'game' to generate a sequence of realistic situations faced with which the participants (the users) would make decisions on what to do, taking account of the new transport facilities available to them.

In the activity model developed for this game most of the information on which users based their decisions came, unlike in most gaming models, from their real life circumstances, – their committments, where they lived, their income etc. This was found to be necessary otherwise users became overloaded with new information and did not know how to react. The other inputs consisted of a number of credible 'expected events', (going to work, holidays, invitations, appointments, etc.), which users were informed of before the simulation run, and various 'unexpected events', (system faults, sickness, weather conditions etc.), which were fed in by game controllers during the run.

Five experiments were attempted, each with a different married couple as participants. Three owned cars, two did not. Each experiment began with an introduction session during which the users were informed of the new facilities available to them. After this introduction they made simulated journeys using each of the new systems until they were familiar with their operation. Induction was followed by an activity simulation run, during which the users had to plan their activities according to their known committments and personal preferences, modifying their plans in response to the unexpected events fed in. When users' plans required a journey, they decided whether the new transport facilities met their requirements by specifying a choice or choices of mode, routes, etc., and working through the details of the journey. Written records and taperecordings were kept of the process and results of users' decision-making. Records were also kept of any other occurrences, such as questions to game-controllers. Simulation runs lasted between three and four hours during which several days of decision-making time were covered. Experiments were concluded with an short discussion in which participants fed back their impressions and ideas.

Some surprising results emerged from these experiments. They are reported here, although they must be highly tentative, to indicate the kind of information obtainable from simulation.

Perhaps the most significant finding was that the users considered that none of the publically-owned systems, (personal transit, town cars and dial-a-bus), either singly or in combination could meet *all* their urban transport needs satisfactorily. One major point of criticism was that to complete many types of journey required one or more changes of mode, or what added up to an unacceptable amount of walking. In particular journeys to outer suburban areas and journeys involving sub-destinations were served unsatisfactorily. To provide a personal transit system offering sufficient flexibility and range to cater for more than just travel to and from work would, it appears, require a prohibitively fine and extensive network of tracks and stop. There was some indication, however, that even a limited network — along existing major public transport routes — would offer a preferred service to the private car and existing modes of public transport for medium and long distance commuting journeys, because of the relatively rapid door-to-door journey times on personal transit offered by moderate average vehicle speeds of 20—30 mph.

Systems for local circulation, (dial-a-bus and self-drive town cars), were not favoured. Dial-a-bus was too slow, while users considered that the effort and expense of hiring a town car for a short journey was not worth while, particularly since they could not be sure that a car would be available when they wanted it.

For drivers, the dual-mode transit system appeared to offer a highly satisfactory system of transport for urban travel. This is hardly surprising since, if a driver has exclusive use of a dual-mode vehicle, the type of service offered closely matches a private car. Users appeared unwilling to hire dual-mode vehicles on a trip basis from local bays without a facility for reserving a vehicle before setting out. This suggests that a booking facility may be a necessary feature of a real system. A dual mode system is of course not available to non-drivers and privately owned vehicles would give rise to similar problems to those caused by private cars. Many users complained that the dual-mode vehicle had insufficient power and range to make journeys to outer urban areas, so they would still wish to have a car of their own. In fact private benefits of the new systems over existing public transport appear insufficient on their own to cause car owners to cease wanting to use their cars in towns, unless legal or financial constraints were imposed. Their major benefits are *social* — reduced congestion, noise, pollution, accidents, etc.

There was no evidence of any drastic changes in travel behaviour caused by the new facilities. This is not really surprising in such short experiments in which users have not had enough time to adapt to the new conditions. However, users did spontaneously 'discover' during the simulation that the personal transit system could be used for eating while travelling and for sightseeing around the town. One couple suggested that the vehicle could make an excellent love nest!

Some of the users were worried about the possible embarrassment or even dangers of sharing a small isolated vehicle with strangers. It should be remembered when planning such systems that this could be a critical deterrent for some users.

It was possible to infer a tentative set of *performance requirements* for an *idealized* form of future urban transport system from the users' decisions, discussions and comments during and after the experiments. These are listed below:

1. *Walking.* In fine weather — up to 1/2 mile. In poor weather or with luggage — a few yards.
2. *Flexibility and range.* Service to all points in city, including outer suburban areas.
3. *Mode-changing.* — Facilities for multi-stage trips within city without mode-changing.
4. *Availability.* Freedom from timetables. On 5-10 minute demand. Facilities for checking availability before setting out.
5. *Journey Times.* Predictable in advance. Moderate average vehicle speeds (20 — 30 m.p.h.).
6. *User Skill.* Available to nondrivers as well as drivers.
7. *Travel Stress.* No need to drive in heavy traffic.
8. *Cost.* Comparable with costs of existing bus travel

The only one of the new systems that could *potentially* provide this performance is a dial-a-ride type of system offering both public self-drive and passenger vehicles of various sizes running on existing roads, (possibly for later conversion to automatic control). The system would have to include an information system via which users could obtain details of vehicle availability and make reservations[12]. Mass transit systems, such as railways guideways, would still be required in large cities in addition to a dial-a-ride service to cope with heavy demands along travel 'corridors'.

Conclusions

The experiments have shown that major errors in man-machine system design can arise if human needs, difficulties and preferences are not investigated prior to system development.

Simulation of future systems using simplified hardware and human participants appears to offer a simple and cheap means of identifying major human needs and difficulties likely to affect the real system before the system is available for testing. Identifying these human variables, at least tentatively, provides a basis from which one can proceed to more sophisticated methods of investigation, such as prototype development and social experimentation.

Use of the technique to discover major shifts in user behaviour and preferences that may be generated by the introduction of new systems would probably require long periods of induction to give participants the chance to get over what may be termed the 'unfamiliarity threshold' and to adapt to the new conditions. Assessing likely social impacts would require many simulation runs with different groups — operators and administrators, for example, as well as users. Given sufficient time for learning and adaptation, the combined effects of multiple changes in the participants' scenario — for example new work patterns, differing income levels and simultaneous access to several new systems — could potentially be investigated. In other words the technique potentially offers a means of bringing a variety of alternative futures into the present for preliminary stage of evaluation.

References and Remarks

1) A.G. Oettinger and S. Marks, Run computer run — the mythology of educational innovation.
Harvard University Press (1969)

2) M.J.E. Cooley, Computer-aided design — its nature and implications, AUEW, (Technical and Supervisory Section, Ouslow Hall, Surrey (1972)

3) T. Gordon, and O. Helmer, Report on a long — range forcecasting study, RAND Corporation, Santa Monica, California, Report P. 2982 (1964)

4) I.D. Illich, Deschooling Society, Calder and Boyars (1970)

5) J. Forrester, World dynamics, Wright-Allen Press Inc. (1971)

6) Project Intrex Staff, Semi — annual activity reports, Massachussetts Institute of Technology, (1966–1970)

7) The term used in A. Spilhaus, Technology, living cities and the human environment. Science, Vol. 162, Decmber (1968)

8) The term used in J.C. Jones, Trying to design the future. Design No. 225 (67)

9) Depending on the system under study, the simulation may involve manipulating the variables in a mathematical model, (assuming that the variables and the relationships between them are known); humans responding to a simulated prototype system, (as in the project reported here); or human players interacting in a 'game', (as in a business game).

10) The project is desribed in full in R. Roy, The future of public services. Unpublished Ph. D. thesis, Design research Laboratory, UMIST, Manchester (1971)

11) These experiments are reviewed in N. Cross, Predicting the effects of computer-aided design systems, in Proceedings of the International Conference on Computers in Architecture, University of York, Sept. (1972) pp 157–166.

12) An evolutionary plan for a traffic system similar in principle to this has been proposed in J.C. Jones, A credible future for city traffic, in Tehnological forecasting. (Edited by R.V. Arnfield Edinburgh University Press (1969)

The Effective Organization of
Social Problem Oriented
Technology Assessment

ORGANIZING FOR TECHNOLOGY ASSESSMENT IN GOVERNMENT

Dieter Schumacher

SYSTEMPLAN e. V.

Institut für Umweltforschung und Entwicklungsplanung

Heidelberg, Federal Republic of Germany

1. Introduction

Technology assessment or at least the philosophy behind it are widely accepted as tools and guidelines for a qualitatively high level of social and societal development [1,2]. It is clear that this general feeling puts pressure on governments and public administration towards establishing suitable institutional mechanisms for technology assessment in the public sector. The question is then, where and how to install these functions and who else, outside government, can be incorporated into these efforts.

2. Constraints

Any major technology assessment process is in principle dealing with a development problem or deficiencies, for which a system of solutions is being searched. This broad spectrum is in permanent conflict with the (inevitable) *divided responsibilities* in public administrations. C. Abt has mentioned [3] that technology is still too much unit instead of systems oriented. So is, in some respect, public administration. Operationally speaking, this means that persons dealing with a given major assessment issue are likely to be members of different ministerial departments competing with each other for problem solutions, budgets, etc. Administrative fragmentation is a major constraint against easy implementation of technology assessment functions, at least as far as the executive branch of governments is concerned.

In addition to this, the public service has, on the average, hardly enough *analytical manpower and motivation* to deal with major assessment issues. We are all aware of the difficulties to staff ministerial planning units and to provide for their impact on the line management. The synthesis of technological, social, economic etc. skills with administrative skills and political sensibility — which appears to be essential for technology assessment — is hard to achieve within governmental assessment teams.

To some extent, the legislative and the executive branches of governments are competitive candidates for being intrusted with technology assessment functions. This conflict is very much related to the constitutional and actual (traditional) balance of power between the branches in each country. See below for further comments.

Constraints as well as opportunities arise from the fact that non-governmental organizations and groups could and should be involved in the assessment process. There is a permanent conflict between the desired impartiality essential for an assessment, and the fact that assessment involves putting value to something, i.e. to weigh a given issue with respect to a value system to be established or defined. There is a wide stress field between impartial assessment and advocacy assessment (which stands for the organized confrontation of different views expressed). One could even take the view that a neutral assessment is not feasible at all.

The latter constraint has a strong impact for the following reasons:

a) If government involves outside institutions in technology assessment, there is not very much choice with respect to impartiality. There are only a few institutions in a country which combine scientific expertise, methodological skills, knowledge of government and public administration, and independence.

b) Due to this scarce potential of independent institutions, governments frequently assign the very producers of the technologies to be assessed to do the assessment, which exposes the latter, of-course, to an embarrassing situation of conflict. In fact, the bulk of assessments of advanced nuclear reactors, high speed ground transportation, urban mass transpotation etc.) have so far been performed by groups adherent to these solutions and having vested interests in these developments.

c) In relation to b), the contracting government runs into the danger of using such expertise − consciously or unconsciously − as an alibi, i.e. placing responsibility on more shoulders.

d) A major problem is the recognition of opinions expressed by those groups who have neither the skills nor the opportunities to participate in technology assessment. Consider transportation issues, for example, where a social balance would call for an 'equal' representation of producers *and* users in the assessment process. The question of participation in technology assessment is clearly a problem not yet solved in a satisfactory manner.

Finally, a major constraint arises from the financial burden connected with assessment studies. In a recent survey of some 100 assessment samples performed in various branches of the United States government, the cost was found to range from $ 100.000 − 400.000 [4].

3. Assessment in legislative vs. executive branch

It has been stated above that this question depends to a large degree on the balance of power in a given country. As far as the United States are concerned, the following pros and cons for location of the Office of Technology Assessment (OTA) in the *legislative* branch have been expressed [5].

Pro legislative branch

− Decision making on important national issues is a prime responsibility of the Congress and Congress is a legitimate representative body for expressing the collective will of the people.

− Major proposals for new technology programmes originate from the executive branch. Hence, Congress needs better tools to probe and assess these programmes before resource allocation.

— For effective legislation, Congress needs an early warning system for negative and long range impacts of technological issues.

— An OTA within the legislative branch could work exclusively according to the specific needs, objectives and functions of Congress. All Committees of Congress would have a common reference board of information and expertise.

Contra legislative branch

— There are other governmental services and committees already existing that could be intrusted with assessment functions in addition to their previous assignments.

— In view of the amount of information sources and channels already existing, it is doubtful whether OTA would succeed in sorting out essential from nonessential information; it may in the worst case enhance the information bias.

— Congress should rather rely on ad hoc panels, National Academies, existing expert staffs, etc.

— Technology assessment is an executive branch function anyway. New demand should be satisfied by expansion of these staffs.

— Assessment priorities involve political, not technical issues. Their determination cannot be delegated to subordinated offices.

— OTA would complicate the legislative process.

This list of pros and cons demonstrates the 'domestic' aspects behind the thinking. Therefore, a general recommendation is not possible, except perhaps that a careful assessment of *existing* institutions, committees etc. as to their eligibility should be done before new capacities are being set up.

It is clear that in the United Stated, Congress is taking a more active part in national decision making than, for example, the legislative bodies in France and the Federal Republic of Germany, for constitutional and other reasons. It's only recently then, that first moves have been done on how to deal with technology assessment. In view of the limited administrative and scientific potential of legislative services in many of our countries, the assessment function should realistically be placed in a central position, serving both legislative and executive needs. The renouncement of duplication of assessment services for legislative and executive branches has, of course, the disadvantage that the control function of the parliament with respect to the programmes of executive agencies is weakened.

In countries with less administrative and institutional resources than the United States, staffs and institutions *outside* government will have an increasing importance. In fact, the technology assessment movement offers in principle quite new and challenging fields of operation for such institutions as ANVAR (Agence Nationale de Valorisation de la Recherche) in France, the Board of Technical Development in Sweden, TNO (Nederlandse Organisatie voor Toegepast Natuurwetenschappelijk Onderziek) in the Netherlands, to give a few examples only. In each case, the implementation of assessment functions requires a careful design of the network of responsibilities and involves a large amount of political sensibility.

4. Assessment within vs. outside Government

V.T. Coates[4] has compiled a list of advantages and disadvantages of in-house vs. contractor assessment, as the results of an empirical inquiry in various government agencies.

The *advantages* of in-house assessment staffs were reported to be

— they had greater credibility for agency management,

— they showed greater likelihood of producing institutional change in the agency,

— individual assessors were protected from constituency pressure by their bureaucratic anonymity,

- the data base remains available to the agency,

- in-house expertise is developed and maintained,

- the assessment activity can be flexibly scheduled in terms of time, resources, and workload.

As *disadvantages* of in-house assessments were named:
- the lack of a multidisciplinary staff in most offices,

- a relative lack of external credibility,

- the possibility of institutional bias,

- the ease of suppression of assessments by administrators displeased by the findings or implications.

The *advantages* of technology assessments performed by *contractors* were reported as:
- there is less institutional bias and greater objectivity,

- they have greater external credibility,

- more disciplines can be used than are present in most agency offices,

- the regular work of the staff can proceed without interference.

As *disadvantages* of having assessment done by contractors it was claimed that
- there are severe difficulties of coordination and management when agency and contractor are geographically separated,

- contractors tend to tell agencies what the agency wants to hear (as the contractor perceives it),

- contractor reports can also be ignored or suppressed by agency management.

The government officials showed a tendency to prefer independent research organizations over university-based groups. As a general conclusion, it was felt that maximum independence and comprehensiveness is gained when

— the assessment is sponsored by a source not directly responsible for the programme or project being assessed, such as the National Science Foundation or the Executive Office of the President, and

— the assessment is performed by a research group which values its reputation for objectivity as a chief stock-in-trade.

It is emphasized that the assessment range reviewed in this Section is only a part of the whole assessment network a nation should establish. Especially the linkage of industry efforts on the one hand[6] and of citizen (group) participation on the other hand to governmental action have not yet really been achieved. Therefore, an optimization of governmental technology assessment is likely to be of a technocratic nature unless the environment of government is well linked to the processes and operations.

5. Some Practical Recommendations

While it is admittedly difficult to design general guidelines on how to organize for technology assessment in government, a few practical thoughts may help to define the actual organizational scheme.

— On a micro-level, a minimum responsibility for and committment to technology assessment should be assigned to any government executive active in technology development programmes. There should be no need to control him by a separate assessment staff. The latter would run into the classical line-staff communication obstacle.

— Large scale assessment studies should — on the other hand — be performed in special governmental units (where a country can afford them), by external groups or by mixed committees. Their efforts take 1-2 years usually, so that a detachment of the staff from other assignments is advisable. The government has to safeguard the inter-dependence of these staffs and protect them from interference by governmental, political or private interest groups.

— The assessment staff should be composed of people who do not know in advance the best alternative solution to the problem at stake. Therefore, in general, they should not be spokesmen of groups involved in the issue. The staff may be exchanged during the study, since different skills and experience may be needed during the course of the assessment process.

— Assessment studies are expensive on a short range point of view, and normally, governments do not have an immediate budget for issues coming up unexpectedly. Assessment, on the other hand, is cheap when the long term return on investment of a government program-me is maximized by the analysis. Finance departments should subscri-be to the guideline that a small percentage of any research and tech-nology budget is worthwhile to be spent for assessment and careful prediagnosis of the issues.

— In organizing for technology assessment, the pluralism inherent in the valuation of social development has to be sustained. If govern-ment sets up its own assessment function, it must also recognize and emphasize (and perhaps even sponsor) assessment by other partners in the national system, namely industry, labour unions etc.

— A practical move of government would consist in demanding some kind of assessment effort in proposals handed in for technology support programmes.

A vital tool for reducing the (national) bias and partiality in techno-logy assessment is an international exchange of studies performed within national constraints. Since all countries of a given structure or state of development are facing comparable problems and issues, they are likely to face similar alternative to solving these problems, and they eventually will assess alternative modes of action with reference to their specific value systems, potentials and resources. A comparative evaluation of these analyses would be of use for all countries involved; it would presumably help to identify manipulations and partialities in individual studies. Furthermore, it would broaden the basis for technology development across boarders. It is clear that international organizations like the Common Market, OECD and the United Nations Economic Commissions could stimulate and moderate this exchange.

In conclusion, emphasis is placed once again on the necessity to carefully design the technology assessment organization for each country, paying tribute to its constitutional framework, to the division of power between the various social groups, and to the specific potentials and resources available.

References

1) See F. Hetman, this Volume

2) See D. Schumacher, this Volume

3) See C. Abt, this Volume

4) V.T.Coates, Technology and Public Policy, The Process of Technology Assessment in the Federal Government, Program of Policy Studies in Science and Technology, The George Washington University, July (1972).

5) Technology Assessment for the Congress, U.S. Congress, Senate, Committee on Rules and Administration, November 1 (1972), United States Government Printing Office, Washington (1972), Appendix B.

6) See papers of D. Altenpohl, and H. Geschka and G.R. Schaude, this Volume

TECHNOLOGY ASSESSMENT IN INDUSTRY

Dieter Altenpohl
Swiss Aluminium
Zürich, Switzerland

1. Why Technology Assessment in Industry?

Most of the planning of technological activities is actively carried out in industry and not by governments or other institutions. We also must remember that the active use of technology is almost exclusively carried out by industry. Therefore I believe that technology assessment really should be done by industry and even before government occupies itself with a specific issue.

As long as industry exists it has fulfilled many useful social functions. Perhaps there has, however, under the so-called capitalistic system, been put too much emphasis on that profit making would be the only purpose of an industrial enterprise. Now, in the early seventies, there is an increasing awareness that making money is a necessary purpose of an industrial enterprise but under certain constraints. One of the main constraints will be in future to provide, on an increasing level of effort, useful services to the public. This is reflected in many recent publications or catch-words, for instance: Industry has to behave like a 'good citizen'. Managing 'to make money while doing good' is one of the main managerial objectives for the forthcoming years. That is the reason why technology assessment is an important instrument for the preparation of management decisions.

Actually industry should be the leader in technology assessment and not governments. A useful example for this is the cooperation of several of the large chemical companies in Europe with regard to environmental questions. These companies have decided to set up standards themselves for chemicals which are now regarded as being bad offenders against environment. Some of these materials are taken or will be taken completely from the market, other will be replaced on a sliding scale by less harmful products, and emission standards will be set by the industry to be submitted to committees which consist of government delegates, people from industry and science to finally approve these standards prepared by industry.

It is well known that the environmental legislation about car emissions went just the other way around, and the car industry is now suffering from government standards which are difficult to fulfill. One of the reasons for this unpleasant situation is that the car companies did not do early enough an intensive technology assessment to arrive at the necessary conclusions and to start corresponding developments even before public and government pressure was clearly evident.

2. How should Technology Assessment be carried out in Industry?

In Figure 1 we have described in a flow-chart the total process of technology planning in a company. This flow-chart is, by intention, kept as simple as possible, to make it digestable also to management which often dislikes too complex systems of organizational measures. As can be seen, technology assessment is a step between the end of the forecasting process and the beginning of the final feasibility study. The technology planning is best taken care of by using all incremental inputs which belong to the technology planning process at the right stage to structure and use them in the right way,

Figure 2 gives two examples, how technology assessment would actually be carried out in a car company or by a prime aluminium producer.

The examples are abbreviated for purpose of easy understanding, but show, that this is a logical sequence to carry out technology planning including technology assessment.

There are many publications on the methodology of technology assessment and we refer here to pertinent recent literature. As an example,

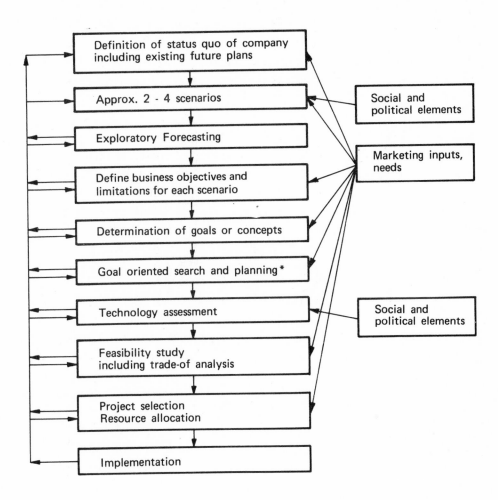

Definition of status quo of company
including existing future plans

Approx. 2 - 4 scenarios

Social and
political elements

Exploratory Forecasting

Marketing inputs,
needs

Define business objectives and
limitations for each scenario

Determination of goals or concepts

Goal oriented search and planning*

Technology assessment

Social and
political elements

Feasibility study
including trade-of analysis

Project selection
Resource allocation

Implementation

*= Normative forecasting

Figure 1: The Process of Technology Planning

Figure 2: Illustrative Examples of the Steps of Technology Planning

Example 1: Automobile Sector   Example 2: Aluminium Sector

1. Status quo – future plans

An automobile-producer wants to stay in individual   A primary aluminium producer wants to strengthen his
transportation business by 1985   position by 1985

2. Scenarios

– zero pollution   – no electrolytic smelters in highly industrialized coun-
                                                             tries because of lack of energy

– lack of fossil fuels   – electrolytic smelters in developing countries possible

– 80 % of materials to be recycled   – recycling will be a main restraint

3. Exploratory Forecasting

possible technical solutions: – Which processes using less energy will be available?
                                                           – in which countries will electrolytic smelters be
– fuel cells   possible?
– new batteries   – what techniques for recycling will be available?
– steam engines
– all Aluminium car
– all plastic car

4. Business objectives and limitations

We can develop an individual transportation system   Aluminium can grow further, if there will be a process
which fulfills the requirements of the scenarios   which uses much less energy than today's processes
                                                           and/or if new smelters are possible in developing coun-
                                                           tries

5. Determination of goals or concepts

. To develop a car with the following features:
— zero pollution
— fuel consumption less than 50 % of today's cars
— recycling of 80 % of the materials must be possible

To find and/or develop a process which uses e.g. less than 10 % energy of today's processes

6. Goal oriented search and planning

Which of the propulsion systems/materials of No 3 have a chance to meet these goals, and which measures have to be undertaken?

Which of the processes described under No 3 will utilize less than 10 % energy?
What will their technical maturity be?

7. Technology Assessment

Analysing all possible side effects, e.g.:
— generation of steam causes too much pollution
— production of plastics is limited because of lack of fossil fuel

What will be the side effects, e.g. pollution influence on working force etc?

8. Feasibilty Study

What will be the overall costs for the various kinds of systems/materials?

What will be the overall costs for the various alternatives of each process?

9. Project selection

Which system/material

Which process or process alternative

will best meet company's marketing, financial, engineering capabilities etc.?

10. Implementation

Figure 3: Seven Major Steps in making a technology assessment.

STEP 1 DEFINE THE ASSESSMENT TASK
Discuss relevant issues and any major problems
Establish scope (breadth and depth) of inquiry
Develop project ground rules

STEP 2 DESCRIBE RELEVANT TECHNOLOGIES
Describe major technology being assessed
Describe other technologies supporting the major techno-
logy
Describe technologies competitive to the major and suppor-
ting technologies

STEP 3 DEVELOP STATE-OF-SOCIETY ASSUMPTIONS
Identify and describe major nontechnological factors influencing the application of the relevant technologies

STEP 4 IDENTIFY IMPACT AREAS
Ascertain those societal characteristics that will be most influenced by the application of the assessed technology

STEP 5 MAKE PRELIMINARY IMPACT ANALYSIS
Trace and integrate the process by which the assessed
technology makes its societal influence felt

STEP 6 IDENTIFY POSSIBLE ACTION OPTIONS
Develop and analyze various programs for obtaining
maximum public advantage from the assessed technologies

STEP 7 COMPLETE IMPACT ANALYSIS
Analyze the degree to which each action option would alter
the specific societal impacts of the assessed technology
discussed in Step 5

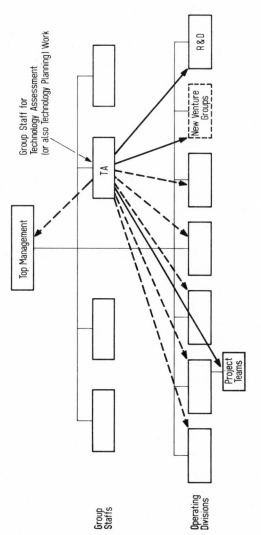

Fig. 4: Technology Assessment Organization in Industry

Figure 3 shows the 7 steps of technology assessment as suggested by the MITRE Corp. in USA.

3. By whom shall Technology Assessment be carried out?

There are many ways how an industrial company can organize for technology assessment. For a large company it is recommended to have one central department or group-staff which is occupied with the total process of technology planning as explained in Appendix 1. As shown in Figure 4, this group-staff has within the company mainly the following receivers for the results of technology assessment:

(1) Project teams who work on a feasibility study within the traditional product range of the company
(2) New venture groups
(3) Research and development institutions
(4) Periodic information should be given to top-management and division managers, regarding important findings about environment and other social impacts (trends, threats, opportunities).

4. Conclusion

(1) In the process of technology planning of industrial companies, technology assessment will have increasing importance.

(2) Industry should be the leader in technology assessment and arrive at positive cooperation with relevant government agencies.

(3) In the process of this development, top-management of industries will increase their awareness, that a main purpose of an industrial company is to serve public interest and that this is an excellent long-range company goal.

(4) In many industries, systematic technology assessment work is in early stages. It is recommended to have first a small special group on corporate level to begin with technology assessment work as an input into the technological and corporate planning.

SOME HYPOTHESES ON TECHNOLOGY ASSESSMENT ORGANIZATION IN INDUSTRY

Horst Geschka and Goetz R. Schaude
Battelle-Institut
Frankfurt, Federal Republic of Germany

During our engagement with innovation processes in studies both for industry and for government we were confronted with various facts which we condensed into two hypotheses:

(1) There is no technology assessment in industry (at present).

(2) Industry *alone* is not in a position to carry out technology assessment.

We will now try to prove these hypotheses:

While basic research is carried out mainly by public institutions (universities, state research institutes, etc.), applied research and development is mostly done in industry. The process of bringing a new technology into practical use, known as 'innovation', is also taking place in industry.

The introduction of a new technology with its direct effects and side-effects has to be decided by a group of decision makers, the management. An investigation to which we referred above on decision making in the innovation process in West-German companies lead us to the conclusion that the organizational and methodological frame-work of internal decision-making is very poor. The evaluation procedures are very rough and subjective. In the majority of the cases there is no real rational assessment of the business chances and risks. In this situation it remains vague where and how to integrate a wide concept of technology assessment. So far our thoughts on hypotheses (1), which was derived from extensive and thorough fieldwork.

Let us now turn over to hypothesis (2):

Another obstacle we see in technology assessment by industry is that assessing new technologies means comparing the possible impacts with a value system. But there is no valid system of objectives, i.e. a system of social indicators. Technology assessment needs, however, ethical, social, political, ecological and humanistic evaluations. For a technology assessment study these possible values and their future evolution have to be forecasted.

But how should industry do this? How are they going to set the standards?

In most companies there do not exist multidisciplinary teams which are required for carrying out technology assessment studies.

The necessity for carrying out a technology assessment study for a single company may only arise every two years. So most of the time the multidisciplinary team would be out of work.

There are other factors, e.g., in some areas knowledge on the basic underlying mechanisms and interrelations are still lacking — like in ecology. Technology assessments must therefore be very tentative.

On the other hand technologies with undesired effects on society may bring business losses to the company involved. Firms not foreseeing these side-effects may come very suddenly to real breakdowns as the example of SST or Contergan show. Therefore private firms are supposed to be interested in a carefully and broad technology assessment by themselves.

The danger is — on the one hand — that the public has to bear the costs of such misdirected developments and, on the other hand, that we load too much responsibility on these single units of the economic system. When individual firms do not foresee — willingly or not — physical or social dangers, disasters may occur.

The clear conclusion is that industry cannot be left alone. New mechanisms must be introduced to ensure that the secondary and tertiary side-effects are taken into consideration before an innovation is launched.

It seems difficult to find adequate mechanisms. Different approaches are possible:

(a) New technologies have to be registered — perhaps in connection with patent application; on choice of a specific technology assessment institution, crucial or important developments are selected and thoroughly assessed.

(b) The firms themselves have to carry out technology assessments or in most cases have it done by competent research organizations. These technology assessments have to be checked and controlled by central institutions:

— There already exist in all states several official institutions supervising technological developments, i.e. for automobiles, drugs, construction, radio-active substances, nuclear and steam power stations etc. (e.g. in Germany the ,,Technischer Überwachungs-Verein''); this technological supervision is presently performed in a very narow sense. The scope of supervision of these bodies can be broadened.

— Industry may establish own self-organized institutions — perhaps on the basis of existing industry-federations — to fulfill the function of supervision of technology assessment studies.

Other forms are possible

In any case an official controlling institution has to be established with the functions:

— development and broadening of a technology assessment methodology

— setting up a system of goals and objectives

— coordination of assessment work

— evaluation of technology assessment studies carried out.

It is evident that such an institution has to be neutral and has to work in close contact to research units of all disciplines.

Efforts have to be undertaken to make the developers (industry) themselves more sensitive to the secondary effects of new technologies in order to encourage them to invest in such a form of research. Perhaps regulations in taxations or subsidies may here be the adequate concepts. It is really a question who has to bear the costs of such studies; today most studies of the character of technology assessment are financed by the state. This may be changed and transferred to industry but with the effect that prices of new socially desired technologies will rise.

Finally, the secondary effects of technology assessment regulations on decision-making in industry itself have to be regarded. In the actual state of decision-making in industry and the poor state of knowledge of value systems, ecological and social interrelations and data technology assessment regulations will surely bring in new uncertainties to the decision-makers and thus discourage their willingness to invest in new technologies. This may especially be true for areas where innovations are socially very desirable. We have to examine such possible effects thoroughly in advance because otherwise technological development may slow down.

Conclusions and Notes

AT THE LIMITS OF ASSESSMENT

Brian Wynne

Science Studies Unit, University of Edinburgh

Edinburgh, Scotland, United Kingdom

This paper was put together at short notice in an attempt to review the presentations and discussions of the meeting so far, and to provide some further questions in the context of the whole meeting.

I think we are all agreed that scientific and rational approaches have contributed much to the beneficial development of man's situation in his natural and social environment, and the wider assimilation into systems of analysis, of sub-systems hitherto ignored or unenvisaged, is a clear advance in our understanding and improvement of diverse and complex social forces. We have seen many examples of such broad approaches in the last three days. However, there are limits to the universal efficacy of the rational systemic approach. In several of the discussions here at S.A.I.N.T., the current and obvious limitations of such a universal systemic methodology of social affairs, have been ascribed more to prototypical difficulties inherent in all innovatory advances, whether social or technical. It remains a moot point whether their ultimate development in scope and sophistication, to provide us with a universally regulated and rationally ordered world, is either feasible or desirable. I would like to suggest that this is the most germane question in the whole area of 'Technology Assessment and Quality of Life'.

So far, the implicit conceptualization of 'Quality of Life' has essentially involved a passive view of man in society. This has shown itself in two fundamental but associated ways:

Firstly, in the hard technological determinism implied in the study of the impact of technology upon man. As Francois Hetman pointed out in his very stimulating paper, to approach technology assessment from the side of technology's impact upon society, implies that man and society merely react to technology, which has somehow an internal logic of its own. The causal links are of course much more complex than this, and are too circuitous to be fully understood, certainly at present. Some things we can say, however. One is that social and technological forces are never completely distinguishable. Technological change is conceived by social forces as much as by any internal objective logic. Again, as Mr. Hetman pointed out, technologically triggered social innovation is a contradiction in itself. It is not technology but men who are responsible for society. The implicit assumption of many papers, of this hard technological determinism, has led us to a rather upside-down view of technology's social role and allowed an almost total neglect of the question of the value content of technology itself in society. To ignore such questions is to address the problems on hand only in a superficial way, and the implications for participatory democratic futures to which we all aspire, are serious.

The assumed view of man as a passive reactor to technology, questionnaires, Clark Abt's social games or whatever, has been consolidated by the technological deterministic approach. To equate quality of life with lack of tension, degree of satisfaction and 'happiness', is to relegate man to the level of the unconscious animal. To ask someone 'how satisfied are you? ' may be to measure 'how well socialized are you? ' To use such methods in assessing quality of life is to ignore the question 'how socialized are you into your existing social predicament? ' can hardly give a positive measure of 'quality of life'. Concepts such as consciousness and freedom, in the sense of active involvement, rather than the passive response and dissolution of tension and restraints, have had little place in our discussions so far. Yet such active consciousness and the internal tensions of existence which such consciousness involves, are surely the essence of life. The kind of technology assessment we have in the main discussed here, seems to be going in the opposite direction — towards, at times, a nakedly behaviourist approach, aiming to reduce the degree of conflict and tension in a situation by providing, or attempting to provide, a universal set of concrete, objective ground rules, by which to escape from the moral and ethical responsibility of coming to a decision on the strengths and weaknesses, prejudices and open social and political ideologies associated with that particular situation.

When used to seek such long-term security in decision making, technology assessment is in danger of becoming a regressive and reactionary tool in society, its − to say the least − uncertain scientific credentials being used to sell it as a social arbiter to a public fed and watered on the self-legitimating value of scientific methods and rationality. The holistic value of technology assessment is superficially appealing, apparently allowing us to take decisions about actual or potential technological innovation. In its very essence, the idea of management incorporates the idea of neutrality. It aspires to smooth functioning as a good, and a goal in itself.

Yet several examples here have illustrated the fallacy of the neutral and holistic claims of social auditing of technology, or a systemic rational operation of our affairs:

(1) Robert Rea acknowledged that alternatives to the basic philosophy underlying the water scheme proposals to be assessed, were not even within his terms of reference.

(2) A pertinent question on the power consumption of the TRANSRAPID transport system was hardly regarded as a relevant consideration in the social audit of the technology of transportation.

Such apparently arbitrary exclusion of quite fundamental factors raises doubts about the neutrality of such assessment. Whose needs exactly does such assessment satisfy? The value-ridden aspect of such attempts to claim and attain an objective conflict-free assessment and reception of such technologies is nakedly evident. We have had other examples. We cannot talk of technology assessment without *first* − and I stress first − talking of value-conflicts, power relations, and socio-political ideologies, and the way in which they feed into both the generation and assessment of technology.

Have we the right to enjoin the radical to grow out of his political naivete in his critique of present technology and his flirtation with future utopias, if we ourselves, in our hard, grown-up world of science policy, refuse to look critically at the social and cultural inputs to the generation of new technology, and the assumptions and power relations which lie at their root? As has already been pointed out, pre- and post-facto technology assessment are very different enterprises. Yet one cannot ignore the first, just because it is more difficult to be scientific in its analysis. We will never unhook ourselves from the uneasy feeling, expressed in much of the literature, that technology does in fact control us, and that we must therefore fight to get back on top, until we include the pre-natal assessment of technology into our field of responsibility.

If any further reference need be made to the deception which we perpetrate upon ourselves as to the objective and universal efficacy of systemic technology assessment, let us think of the predicament of the underdeveloped nations on planet earth. Except for one or two references, we have almost totally ignored the situation and the fate of other cultures than our own, and Louis Turner has pointed out that they may have some things to teach us about forms of technology more appropriate to a flexible and diverse cultural future.

Whether we talk, though, of 'megatechnology' or alternative technology, it is fallacious to start at the technology end and then to see how society can best be arranged. We have been discussing the prevailing forms of technology (and implicit within this discussion, within the framework of the prevailing values and power-relations) in our own small part of the world, albeit a part with a grossly over-grown worldwide influence. Even within this partial perspective, we have in the main discussed technology assessment in a limited and deterministic way. To claim a universal certificate of approval, whether now or after future refinements, for such an ethnocentric and value-ridden process as the technology assessment we have been describing here, is, I think, to court the ridicule of anyone with an active critical mind.

I would like to suggest that the major challenges to us in technology assessment lie in technology's relation to social, economic and political power groupings, and in developing a finely-tuned sensitivity to the capabilities, but more importantly, the limitations of systemic technology assessment and social auditing, in each social situation as it arises.

We ought perhaps to be looking less for closed-ended solutions and concrete guidelines for complex problems, which, if man is to retain any quality of life, must demand an element of uncertainty, tension and open-endedness, and ask us to make open and acknowledge moral and political judgements in an often conflict-full situation.

We cannot impose our own ideas of happiness or quality upon other social groups, cultures or nations in a blaze of paternalistic benevolence. To define quality of life is luckily impossible. We cannot abstract quality of someone's life, and then optimize it, from our own culture- and biographically-bound standpoint. 'Situations' do not possess the characteristics of objectivity. Consequently, certainty does not arise from the mere understanding of objectively existing or describable phenomena. Even the adequate knowledge of all objectively given facts, such as are provided by empirical research and scientific means, can't fully encompass the perspective as seen from a man involved in a particular situation. Thus, our ambition to improve the lot of mankind by allegedly 'scientific' and 'value-free' management of his unhappiness, conflicts and neuroses, is a misplaced one. In attempting this, and in ignoring or relegating to secondary importance, the power relations and vested interest relations of technology implementation and technological innovation, we move closer to social behaviourism and in the opposite direction from facing the world's real problems and the question of human development.

To summarize, we have mainly here discussed technology assessment and quality of life within the framework of existing social and power relations, and on the assumption that these be maintained and strengthened by the refinement of their means. If we are seriously to address quality of life as a problem, we must entertain the possibility of fundamental changes in social structures and power relations, and recede from the desire for a concrete future. We cannot therefore afford to assume that technology assessment and the development of assessment techniques, will lead man inexorably to a better world. Discussed in a political vacuum, technology assessment is merely in danger of being used to refine and prolong the existence of inequality, exploitation and inhumanity, rather than, as we would all hope, to improve the quality of human life.

AN 'ASSESSMENT' OF THE CONFERENCE OUTCOME

Louis Turner
Department of Sociology, University of Salford
Salford, Lancashire, United Kingdom

Summing up and closing a conference is a thankless task. If it was good, everyone knows and, unless you are brilliant, your thoughts will be an anti-climax. If it was bad, you run the risk of mortally wounding all the speakers and organisers by saying so. This conference, however, fell somewhere in between these two extremes. It raised most of the right questions, without presenting the definitive analysis of the subject matter.

Technology assessment should be seen in historical perspective. Though Congressman E.Q. Daddario and persons around him may have thrown the term into the public arena, the belief that technology should be the servant of Man and not his master is an old one dating back to well before the Luddites. In any case, we have been assessing one or two technologies for some time. For instance, the 1938 Federal Food, Drug and Cosmetic Act in the United States forced manufacturers of new drugs to show evidence of safety (though not of usefulness) before they could be sold to the public. Rachel Carson, again, was not complaining in *The Silent Spring* that the agro-chemical companies were not doing clinical testing. She was pointing out, rather, that their testing failed to look at dangers to the rural environment as a system. Today's would-be technology assessors take Rachel Carson's thinking a few steps further. They argue that we have failed to see the impact that many technologies have had on social and physical systems which we are often only partly able to understand. The job of the technology assessor is to gather what evidence there is, so that decision makers (whoever they may be) can choose between options with a clear idea of the full implications of the choices open.

However, the new thing about technology assessment is not its philosophy, which is standard to any conference held on futurology or the environment, but the fact that it is trying to put this novel way of approaching technology into practice. This conference, unfortunately, was fairly weak when looking at the efforts of practical technology assessors. We did have a very clear and useful paper from Robert Rea on the work of Abt Associates. The examples he picked, like the choice of a new water supply for Boston, showed very well just how complex any such analysis must be. As well as listing the straight economic and technical issues, they also had to try to assess the impact which various schemes might have on rather more intangible, social indicators like the 'cohesiveness' of various communities.

Interesting as cases like this were, we really missed a good overview of the variety of technology assessment which is taking place at this moment in the United States, Europe and Japan. For instance, the National Environmental Policy Act of 1969 has been crucial in stimulating a number of major studies. The biggest has been the 8 million Dollar study of the Alaskan oil pipeline, which has now been delayed two years while the issues are appealed all the way up to the United States Supreme Court. Again, what are the implications of the S.S.T. debate — how good was the evidence produced? How did the politicians draw conclusions in the face of conflicting evidence from a scientific community which was far from united? There has also been the lengthy debate in Britain about the siting of the third London airport. This decision has an impact not only on the future of rural churches and the nesting grounds of rare geese (how do you quantify such issues?), but will also affect the future development of the whole of South East England, including London.

The common factor in all such studies is that we now look at the impact these new technologies have on the whole environment, which includes not just physical well-being but the quality of life and social relationships. These new factors are extremely difficult to measure or even analyze, and the conference dealt well with the issues in its debate on how to integrate an awareness of the quality of life into the whole of technology assessment. The keynote was struck in the introduction by Gerhard Stöber who went out of his way to stress that the quality of life is what people think it is, and not what remote technocrats guess it is from the arbitrarily existing indicators available to them. It was pointed out in discussion that OECD is unable to produce a comprehensive index of such indicators because governments are only really interested in those which are not going to show their societies in too bad a light. In other words, there is a danger that planners who are just beginning to accept that GNP is no longer an adequate measure of the quality of life, may merely switch to a reliance on new indicators which measure various aspects of physical well-being (life expectancy, consumption of cars, television sets, etc.) but which do not really allow us to draw valid conclusions about the psychological satisfaction that individuals may actually get from such factors.

It was interesting, therefore, to hear three or four papers which concentrated on what people actually perceived as contributing to the quality of life. John Hall's survey research work is the kind of pioneering work which must be done to give technology assessors more confidence when judging the relative weight people put on conflicting variables (i.e. noise from a near-by airport, as against shorter distances to work or greater leisure time). Ruud Bruyn's paper was in much the same social-psychological tradition, though concentrating more on work satisfaction. Paul Drewe put these survey research techniques into focus with an exhaustive look at all the various devices available to assessors for measuring how people will react to various new technologies. If one lesson came from such studies, it was that differing structures of society may have different reactions to a given factor-a phenomenon which will tend to confuse technology assessors who find it desirable to give a clear, unequivocal value to indicators like 'cost benefit of saved travel time'. It could well be that some assessments may end up with two sections of the community wanting quite different solutions. Paul Drewe, for instance, discussed the goal survey of the Los Angeles master plan which showed that wealthy, white suburbanites valued things like a noisy environment or job opportunities significantly differently from poor blacks. This poses a problem for technology assessors which I discuss later in this paper.

Social scientists will thus get sucked (increasingly) into the assessment process, though there is no certainty that many of them are yet ready for this. Clark Abt pointed out just how young a discipline sociology still is, with most of its development having taken place since 1945, and he was backed up implicitly in this by the paper from James Wilson who had criticisms of the usefulness of classically trained economists.

Another strong point in this conference was the attention given to the industrial aspect of technology assessment. There was some scepticism about this, particularly from Vary Coates who found this emphasis very 'European'. She felt that Americans in the field tended to place the major role on government. But this is to gloss over the fact that private corporations are still a major driving force in our society. The search for profits ensures a steady stream of technical innovations. Anyone who knows the Concorde story will vouch for the commercial factors which led to the development of this SST with virtually no serious analysis of its overall acceptability. Again, the drive of the oil companies into the environmentally-treacherous area of offshore exploration and production is a development which needs extremely close assessment.

To some extent companies can do assessment themselves, but only once they are aware of the environmental constraints they work in. Johannes Mak discussed the case of his own company, Hoogovens (the Dutch steel company) which as late as 1965 did not really believe that environmental pressures would hurt them. And yet, within four years, they were forced to cancel a 'green field' steel plant which they planned with the German company, Hoesch, on the Dutch coast. B.A.S.F. was similarly surprised by the strength of environmental opposition when it planned a new plant in Delaware. Even the oil companies (as mentioned earlier) have been taken aback by the success of the opposition to their Alaskan pipeline. Financial calculations which assumed the pipeline would be speedily built have had to be scrapped or revised.

Dieter Altenpohl from Swiss Aluminium felt that industry should be left to police itself — a view which the majority of the conference probably did not accept. This scepticism showed itself further when Dieter Haseke from Krauss-Maffei made a presentation of his company's magnetic lift and aerocushion trains, which are being developed for the urban and inter-city transport needs of tomorrow. There was a feeling amongst questioners that, though they did not deny the need for transport developments for these markets, they did not see that the company had really carried out any technology assessment of note.

The alternative approach was put forward by Horst Geschka and Goetz R. Schaude who argued that assessment standards had to be set and supervised by independent agencies like the Food and Drug Administration in the States. This approach was considered more acceptable by most delegates, but we missed a discussion of the dilemma that tougher environmental safeguards has posed some industries. Pharmaceutical companies, for instance admit the need for improved contraceptive technologies, but they increasingly argue that the time-lag needed for testing new versions is such that the whole process is now uneconomic. They claim that it can take ten years from the discovery of a potential contraceptive to its final clearance for unrestricted public sale. A delay as long as this will make the initial research totally uneconomic since the profits are so far into the future as to be virtually totally discounted. Now, it is quite possible that the pharmaceutical industry's special pleading should be treated sceptically, but technology assessment is an extra delaying factor, and delays can play havoc with the planning of firms which have to make profits if they are to survive. This would suggest that governments may either have to subsidize the expense of technology assessment in certain industries, or else ensure that this kind of research is carried out in State organizations.

Ruud Bruyns' work on work motivation also raised some questions which deserved further discussion. He shows, for instance, that different workers weight things like job satisfaction and promotion prospects in different ways. One can extend his field of interest a little further to argue that the industrial process itself needs assessing, just like any technology which it produces. There is after all, the whole job enrichment movement which in effect assumes that the oldtime assembly line is dehumanizing. General Motors has been discovering that its current workers are rebelling against such work technology (the Lordstown strike has been followed by similarly motivated industrial action in other G.M. plants). It could therefore be that companies will find themselves taking a much more open-minded attitude to the kinds of work-technology they impose on their workforce. Philips, for instance, has been experimenting with alternative assembly techniques both for its European and its Third World employees.

Some sectors of the conference felt that technology assessors should place very much more emphasis on developing such alternative technologies. (Brian Wynne's paper expresses this argument clearly). They feel that technology assessment is too much a part of the existing system. One example of their thinking came when Robert Rea was discussing Boston and its water supply and there was some sharp questioning to see to what extent the assessors had considered a strategy in which Boston consciously cut down on its use of water, instead of merely accepting that the need for more water from outside the city boundaries would continue to rise for the forseeable future. This line of questioning was supported by Anders Ejerhed's paper where he consciously supports the reduction and decentralisation of large cities by the use of improved, conventional rail transport.

These critics who call for the development of more appropriate technologies undoubtedly have a point. It would be a mistake, though, to underestimate the number of problems still left in our society where existing technologies, if applied, would be quite adequate. Clark Abt gave an example from when his company looked into the low-income housing market in the United States. He found that the basic problem was not the state of housing technology, but the multitude of political boundaries affecting single cities, which stifle the kind of initiative which might get decent housing to the people who need them. The technology assessor, in other words, works within an existing political system which, as long as it survives, has the ultimate say over which alternative is finally selected for action. Obviously, the good, socially responsible technology assessor will put forward as many creative alternatives as he can, but he cannot, by himself, dictate which choice should be made. What he can do is point out that obsolete political structures are hindering the introduction of socially desirable technologies, or point out that certain institutions like say the multinational companies, which John Leslie-Miller discussed, are producing the wrong products. There is no reason why a political or non-political organization should not be 'assessed' for its overall impact, just like a technology. There might be the need for a new term, 'social assessment', but the philosophy behind it would be just the same.

The conference never really got round to discussing how one choses a particular technology for study. We've seen just how expensive a major study can be, so one wonders what criterion one would use in deciding to allocate such resources to one innovation rather than another. Again, once one has decided this, how does one decide what is relevant to the assessment, and what is not? Suppose one was assessing DDT when it was still in the laboratory stage. One would obviously have done more extensive clinical trials and recomended that it be used in rather more specific ways than it was in practice. However, given the fact that its use against mosquitos etc. was an urgent social priority, would one still have approved its immediate use, with all its unfortunate ecological side effects? It's difficult to answer this, but one suspects the answer would have been 'Yes' in certain problem areas. For instance, the World Health Organization is still forced to use DDT in its anti-Malaria campaign, until the companies can come up with some improved, safer chemical. The lives to be saved by the campaign are weighed against the known side-effects. However, how much effort would one have put into examining more remote effects like the creation of the population expolosion that we are now facing as the 'DDT generation' starts to multiply in its own turn? This effect has been just as much a problem to the world as DDT traces in the ocean, but would the policy makers of 1945 have acted in any different way if they had been able to foresee the full implications a generation afterwards?

Or to take a contemporary example-would one bother with assessing the introduction of video-recorders? One can make a very strong case arguing that they will destroy the only remaining universal cultural experience a nation now has-its television services, just as the coming of the record player and the long-playing record has led to the rapid disintegration of aural cultures into a wide number of sub-cultures, each with its own music. One can therefore argue that the video-recorder, with its visual version of the long-playing record, will significantly increase the fragmentation of our society. This may be good or this may be bad, but it will certainly make society much harder to manage. So, the question we probably failed to ask ourselves was, how do we decide how much assessment each innovation needs? Some innovations like the SST and the oil pipeline are so vast in size that they choose themselves-but if the body in charge of allocating technology assessment missions is short of of money, how does it choose? One suspects that in the medium term the choice will be made on grounds of political expediency-any group shouting loudly enough will get listened to. This is worrying since there is obviously a high degree of selfishness in many of the existing protests. Nobody wants a power station or a new airport on their doorstep, though most people still want what such investments imply. Clark Abt made this point in his paper when he argued that we have still not come to the point where society really has to make critical choices. We, in the advanced economies, can get rid of some of our polluting industries by 'exporting' them to Third World economies who want the jobs. What we cannot do for long is to slow down the rate at which airports or electricity generating plants are built to a level where current levels of demand will be unsatisfied, without having to eventually face some extremely awkward political choices. So, if technology assessment remains ideologically neutral, it will have a valuable role to play when choices eventually do have to be made.

ON THE AUTHORS

Clark C. Abt
Studied natural and social sciences (PhD). He is President and Treasurer of Abt Associates Inc., Cambridge, Massachusetts.

Dieter Altenpohl
Studied metallurgy and physics in Göttingen. He was associated with Aluminium-Walzwerk Singen, Germany, with Consolidated Aluminium Corp., Jackson, Tenn., and since 1960 with Alusuisse Zürich. He is now director of perspectives and coordination in the Alusuisse headquarters.

Rudolph A. C. Bruyns
Studied sociology of industry at the Catholic University of Nijmwegen, Netherlands, and received a masters degree in 1966 and a PhD in 1972. From 1966 till August 1972 he has been employed in the Psychology Service and Labor Conduct Departments of Dutch State Mines. He is now lecturing at the Frederik Muller Academy Amsterdam.

Paul Drewe
Received a PhD in economics and sociology at the University of Cologne, Germany. He is now Head of the Economic — Sociological Research Section of the Netherlands Economic Institute, Rotterdam, Netherlands. His major publications were focussed on urban and regional planning, migration problems and employment issues.

Anders G. Ejerhed
Is a mechanical engineer by training. He has earlier managed rationalization projects at the Institute for the Planning and Rationalization of Health and Social Welfare Services, Stockholm. Commissioned by the Government, he participated in organizing the new faculty of technology in Lulea, Sweden. He is currently heading the Research Division of the Swedish Association of Engineers and Architects, Stockholm, Sweden.

Manfred Fischer

Received a PhD in physics and mathematics and gained ten years of research experience in plasma physics and electromagnetic wave propagation. Since 1969 he applied systems analysis to problems of R&D planning and to environmental pollution, first with Battelle Institut Frankfurt, now with the Institut für Systemtechnik and Innovationsforschung Karlsruhe of the Fraunhofer Gesellschaft zur Förderung der angewandten Forschung.

Horst Geschka

Graduated 1963 as Dipl.-Wirtschaftsingenieur from the University of Darmstadt and wrote a PhD thesis on the management of R&D. Since 1969 he is Division Head of Battelle Institute Frankfurt and a lecturer at the University of Darmstadt.

Nadezda Grubor

Is a research fellow at the Institute of International Politics and Economics, Belgrade, Yugoslavia.

John F. Hall

Read classics and then social anthropology at Gonville & Cains College, Cambridge, United Kingdom (BA 1963, MA 1967). He obtained a Diploma in Education at St. Cuthberts Society, Durham in 1964. After teaching liberal studies at Openshaw Technical College, Manchester, he was a research assistant at the University of Salford and a lecturer in the postgraduate Department of Transportation and Environmental Planning at the University of Birmingham. Since 1970 he is associated with the Survey unit of the Social Science Research Council London as research fellow and responsible for computer analysis and the social indicator programme.

Dieter W. Haseke

Studied economics at the University of Munich and received a PhD in 1971. He is currently associated with Krauss-Maffei AG Munich and is heading the Group Management and Commercial Administration, Trackbound High-speed Transport Systems.

François Hetman
Obtained a PhD in economic sciences. He has been specializing on economic growth problems and futures research and is currently principal administrator at the OECD Directorate for Scientific Affairs. (The opinions expressed by the author are not necessarily those of the organization to which he belongs).

John Leslie-Miller
Is a member of the Council of the Dutch Confederation of Trade Unions, deputy member of the Dutch Social Economic Council and lecturer at the Institute of Social Studies, The Hague, Netherlands.

Peter Milling
Studied management science and business administration at the University of Mannheim, Germany, and at the Massachusetts Institute of Technology. He received a PhD at the University of Mannheim. He was a member of the Club-of-Rome Research Team at M.I.T. and is now back at the Industrieseminar of the University of Mannheim.

Robert Rea
Studied engineering and is now Vice-President in the Technology Management Area of Abt Associates, Inc., Cambridge, Massachusetts, USA

Jürgen Reichling
Studied biology, chemistry and physics at the University of Heidelberg and received a PhD in 1972. He is currently a research fellow at the Botanical Institute of the University, working on plant physiology and human ecology.

Robin Roy
Received a B.S. in mechanical engineering and MS and PhD in Design Technology. He is now lecturer in design at the Faculty of Technology, the Open University, Bletchley, United Kingdom.

Goetz R. Schaude
Studied mining engineering at the University of Aachen. Subsequently he was a sales engineer with ICI Deutschland, Frankfurt, and is now a

member of the research unit for innovation and creativity at the Battelle Institute Frankfurt.

Dieter Schumacher

Studied physics in Tübingen and Stuttgart (PhD 1965) and political sciences at the Institut d'Etudes Politiques Grenoble. He served as collaborateur etranger at the Centre d'Etudes Nucleaires Grenoble, as assistant to the general manager of Dornier System GmbH Friedrichs-hafen, and as a science advisor and member of the Planning Staff in the Federal Chancellor's Office Bonn. He is now director of SYSTEMPLAN e.V., Institut für Umweltforschung und Entwicklungsplanung, Heidelberg and lecturer at the University of Mannheim.

Gerhard J. Stöber

Studied economics and social sciences in Munich, Frankfurt and Basel (PhD). He was associated with Siemens AG Munich, with the Institut für Sozialforschung, University of Frankfurt, and with the Institut für Stadt- und Landesplanung, University of Karlsruhe. He was then senior research fellow in the Studiengruppe für Systemforschung Heidelberg and a member of the Planning Staff in the Federal Chancellor's Office Bonn. He is now director of SYSTEMPLAN e.V., Institut für Umwelt-forschung und Entwicklungsplanung, Heidelberg, and since 1967 Presi-dent of SAINT.

Louis Turner

Studied psychology at the University of Oxford and was then a research fellow in the Department of Sociology, Salford University. Hi is now with the Royal Institute of International Affairs, London.

James S. Wilson

received a B.Sc. and a MA in economics. From 1966–1972 he was a lecturer in Economics at the University of Strathclyde, Glasgow and is now Senior Lecturer at the Glasgow College of Technology.

Brian E. Wynne

Read natural sciences at the University of Cambridge and completed his Doctorate there in materials science in 1971. He is presently SSRC Research Fellow at the Sciences Studies Unit of the University of Edinburgh, United Kingdom.

ON SAINT

SAINT stands for „Salzburg Assembly: Impact of the New Technology"
which was founded in 1967 as an international, so far mainly European-
based association of individual and corporate members, professionally
interested and experienced in the field of science and technology
policies and the impact of technological innovation on society.

SAINT came into existence as an offshoot of the Salzburg Seminar in
American Studies, located at Schloss Leopoldskron, Salzburg, Austria.
This independent, non-profit organization, having its home office in
Cambridge, Massachusetts, USA, is bringing together, since more than
25 years, American and European experts of many professions and
occupations for work sessions, each lasting three or four weeks, on
major topics of common interest. In summer of 1967 a first session on
„The Impact of Technology on Society" was held. The participants felt
the need for a reunion-type organization which would keep them in
touch with further developments in this vital field and could initiate
concrete projects of international cooperation. It was decided to make an
experiment and to create SAINT.

SAINT is today a self-financing, not overly formal body, officially
chartered in Salzburg, Austria. Although it developed from the Salzburg
Seminar and is still related to this organization in some respects, it is
totally autonomous. Membership is open now to anyone who is involved
and seriously engaged in theoretical or practical questions and problems of
science and technology policy. Hitherto members of SAINT come from
about 20 European countries as well as from other quite different parts of
the world like the United States or India. The list of members includes
experts with a record of achievement from the scientific community, but
also industrialists, government officials, representatives of public administration, of international organizations and the media.

SAINT provides a forum for the exchange of both information and opinion, and for the coordination of research and other activities on problem areas like

- Analysing social and environmental effects of new technologies
- Directing technology to unmet human needs
- Setting long range goals and priorities for technological development
- Measuring and assessing the social costs and benefits of technological applications
- Organizing the process of planning and decision making in technology policy.

From 1968 to 1972 four General SAINT-Conferences were held at Schloss Leopoldskron which provides a unique and stimulating environment for unconventional and lively symposia. Besides these, two Special Conferences were organized on ,,The Organization of Industrial Research and Development" (Birmingham, United Kingdom, 1969) and ,,The Multinational Corporation and its Environment" (Salzburg, Austria, 1971). All Conferences are also open to participants and speakers who are not registered members of SAINT. Prominent as well as less prominent people are encouraged to present papers for discussion.

The greater part of the material presented at the 4th General Conference is compiled in this volume. The 5th General Conference to be held in 1973 will deal with ,,The Vulnerability of our Technological Society" (see announcement on the next page).

S.A.I.N.T.

Salzburg Assembly — Impact of the New Technology

PRELIMINARY ANNOUNCEMENT

5th General SAINT Conference
September 15–19, 1973
Schloss Leopoldskron, Salzburg, Austria

Conference Theme:

'THE VULNERABILITY OF OUR TECHNOLOGICAL SOCIETY'

Does technology carry the seeds of its own destruction? To what extent can dissident groups bring our techno-structure to a halt? What is the relationship of technology to the 'counter-culture'? Is our technology too big and inflexible? What are the alternatives? Do other cultures have more intelligent ways of approaching technology?

These and other questions which are both topical and still relatively little analysed are to be dealt with during the Conference, based on critical evaluation of recent events and case studies.

The broad range of topics which is expected to be covered is tentatively divided into five main sections:

1. Problems: Technological accidents and disasters
2. Problems: Social resistance against or related to technology
3. Solutions: Alternative technologies
4. Solutions: Attempts at social engineering and social control
5. Conclusion: Vulnerability or sensitivity of the system?

Formal presentations of papers will be reduced to a minimum. The Conference will achieve its outcome preferably by intensive dialogues and guided group discussions, relying on a series of preparatory papers with clearly described facts, hypotheses, and arguments. The detailed Conference Programme is available on request. Participation is restricted to about 60 people.

For further information and registration apply to Mr. Louis Turner, Secretary of SAINT, c/o Royal Institute of International Affairs, Chatham House, 10 St James Square, London SW1Y 4LE, United Kingdom.